GW00392412

What an exciting and timely book! G
only make a compelling case for revivi
theologian thought leaders. They also
leadership—much needed today!—ca
which the present day churches are call

Richard Mouw

Academically trained pastors, like engineers or lawyers, may struggle to navigate between a vocation and passion as scholars on the one hand and as practitioners on the other. Of course, not all are called to be both. But Hiestand and Wilson challenge their North American evangelical readership to confront a double problem of anemia—in their churches' theology and in the theological academy's understanding of the church. All those alert to the tension are here invited to a practically minded vision of the pastor as "ecclesial theologian," called to feed his or her people with the life-giving gospel as transforming nourishment for heart and mind.

Markus Bockmuehl, professor, Keble College, University of Oxford

In an age of leadership drawn from business management and results measured solely in numbers, it is wonderfully refreshing to find a clarion call for the return of the pastor theologian. Of course, our authors know that Paul not only thought and wrote, but planted churches and preached—but most of the temptations in our age, far from turning us into thinkers abstracted from people, sound the siren call of mere activism. This book, rightly absorbed, will improve our preaching and help our churches mature, not so much as ends in themselves but as the by-product of loving God with our minds.

D. A. Carson

The Pastor Theologian may be a small book, but it is an ambitious one. Gerald Hiestand and Todd Wilson summon the church to return to a time when pastors were theologians and theologians pastors, when pastors served as *intellectual* shepherds of the church. The renewal of what they call ecclesial theology will provide a needed transfusion into theologically anemic pastoral ministry and pastorally anemic theology.

Peter Leithart, President, Theopolis Institute, Birmingham, Alabama

Most of the best theologians in the history of the church worked as pastors. But sadly, this is not true today. Most pastors now spend the bulk of their time on mundane issues, leaving intellectual ministry to specialists in the academy—who all too often work in a way that is lost on the laity. This is a tragedy indeed. Who is feeding God's people solid theological food (Hebrews 5:12–14)? Kudos to Pastors Hiestand and Wilson for focusing on this problem, and for recommending practical steps that all of us can take—in our churches and our schools—to find a better way forward, helping Christians come to know the Lord we say we love so much.

Douglas A. Sweeney, St. Mark Lutheran Church, Lindenhurst, Ill.,
Trinity Evangelical Divinity School, Deerfield, Ill.

Authors Gerald Hiestand and Todd Wilson demonstrate that the overarching need of today's church is theologians who wear the clerical mantle—"who work and write as those who bear the weight of souls upon their shoulders." The case that they present is winsome and utterly convincing, as they trace the history of the rise and demise of the pastor-theologian, and the resulting theological and ethical anemia of the church. But more, they provide us with a nuanced profile of the ecclesial theologian and a reasoned way forward. *The Pastor Theologian* is an exhilarating and heartening book—and a must-read for the church and the academy where it will produce lively, ministry-changing discussion!

R. Kent Hughes, Senior Pastor Emeritus of College Church,
Wheaton, Ill.

Context matters. A pastor who daily faces the challenges and possibilities involved in leading his or her congregation may see things differently than, and develop insights different from, an academic who faces the challenges of classroom teaching and specialized research. Hiestand and Wilson here argue, accordingly, that a revival of pastorally situated theology may provide resources for the renewal for theology and church alike. The result is a clear, compelling vision, clearly and compellingly stated. A welcome book!

Kevin W. Hector, Assistant Professor of Theology and of the Philosophy
of Religions, The University of Chicago Divinity School

If you're looking for canaries in the church's coal mines, consider our seminaries and divinity schools. In some cases, the seminary has simply become one more outpost of the academy, hijacked by the ideals of the research university, almost allergic to pastoral formation. In other cases, the seminary is reduced to a management seminar where the pastorate is confused with technique. *The Pastor Theologian* is an antidote to both, a vision for ecclesial theology and a theological ecclesia. We need this book because we need pastor theologians.

> **James K. A. Smith,** Calvin College, author of *Desiring the Kingdom*
> and editor of *Comment* magazine

Hiestand and Wilson shine a spotlight on a seismic fault whose damage to the church has been under the radar: the great divorce between the pastoral ministry and academic theology. They argue compellingly that a healthy church body needs red blood (pastoral energy) and gray brain cells (theological intelligence) to grow into Christian maturity. This is a book written in faith — the kind of faith that moves institutional mountains and raises, if not the dead, then at least defunct concepts — like the pastor theologian.

> **Kevin J. Vanhoozer,** Research Professor of Systematic Theology,
> Trinity Evangelical Divinity School

This book is a timely reminder and challenge that pastors, not professors, are the theological leaders of the church. This book is informed by centuries of church history as well as by Scripture and by insightful analysis of the state of the church today. A must-read for anyone seeking guidance on how to bridge—or rather, destroy—the pastor-theologian divide.

> **Simon Gathercole,** Senior Lecturer in New Testament Studies,
> Fitzwilliam College, University of Cambridge

Hiestand and Wilson call pastors and academics to embrace the highest goal for their work: the building up of Christ's body, the church. Their assertion that pastors must have a high level of devotion to Christ, theology, and pastoral work is much needed today, an era in which many churches are dying for lack of knowledge of God and his ways.

> **Paul House,** Professor of Divinity, Beeson Divinity School

Here is a clarion call, not for pastors to take theology more seriously, but to become theologians themselves, *ecclesial* theologians, whose vocation, *as pastors*, is to "traffic in ideas" and to provide a "thought leadership" which are not only biblically based, historically informed, theologically potent, intellectually credible, and culturally relevant, but also, and above all, church-born-and-bred, like the vision set forth in the book itself. Here then is a manifesto to overcome the anemia caused by the disastrous division of labor between church and academy, in which "there is an insufficient amount of ecclesial substance to our theology and theological substance to our churches." Take up and read!

Scott Hafemann, Reader in New Testament, Director of Taught Postgraduate Studieam St. Mary's College, University of St Andrews

The Pastor
Theologian

RESURRECTING AN
ANCIENT VISION

Gerald Hiestand and
Todd Wilson

FOREWORD BY TIMOTHY GEORGE

ZONDERVAN

The Pastor Theologian
Copyright © 2015 by Gerald Hiestand and Todd Wilson

This title is also available as a Zondervan ebook. Visit www.zondervan.com/ebooks.

Requests for information should be addressed to:
Zondervan, 3900 *Sparks Dr. SE, Grand Rapids, Michigan 49546*

Library of Congress Cataloging-in-Publication Data

Hiestand, Gerald, 1974 –
      The pastor theologian : resurrecting an ancient vision / Gerald Hiestand and
Todd Wilson.
           pages   cm
      ISBN 978-0-310-51682-8 (softcover)
      1. Pastoral theology. I. Title.
BV4011.3.W486 2015
253 – dc23   2015001986

While we, the authors of this work, have predominantly used conventional male pronouns in referring to pastors and theologians in general, we fully recognize that ours is the greatest era of women in those fields. No gender assumptions are intended.

Any Internet addresses (websites, blogs, etc.) and telephone numbers in this book are offered as a resource. They are not intended in any way to be or imply an endorsement by Zondervan, nor does Zondervan vouch for the content of these sites and numbers for the life of this book.

Cover design: *Tammy Johnson*
Cover photo: *Masterfile*
Interior design: *Kait Lamphere*

Printed in the United States of America

16 17 18 19 20 21 22 23 24 25 /DCI/ 20 19 18 17 16 15 14 13 12 11 10 9 8 7 6 5 4 3 2

To the Fellows of the Center for Pastor Theologians

Contents

Foreword

By Timothy George

In 1623, the Puritan theologian William Ames published *The Marrow of Sacred Divinity*. This became the first theology textbook used at Harvard College when it was founded a decade later. It contains the best definition of theology I have ever found: *Theologia est scientia vivendo Deo*, which, roughly translated, means, "Theology is the knowledge of how to live in the presence of God."

Why do I like Ames's definition so much? Because it brings together two elements often held at arm's length in the history of the church: the idea that theology is an orderly body of knowledge—a "science," to use the Latin root—and the fact that this body of knowledge has a divinely intended purpose, namely, to enable us to live every moment of our lives with joy and intentionality in the presence of the true and living God. To focus on one without the other is to be a half-Christian. Theology divorced from life is arid intellectualism. A Christian life not based on sound principles will end up in sterile activism or sentimental fluff.

The Pastor Theologian is a brief but potent book that deals with another false dichotomy, one with serious detrimental effects in the life of the church today. Can a Christian minister be both a pastor and a theologian? The two nouns in the title of this book indicate that the normative answer to this question ought to be yes. And yet, this historic vision of pastoral identity has been undermined from two directions. One is the devolution of theology itself as a serious enterprise for every Christian (in the sense of Ames's definition), and the other is the vocational pressure pastors face to devote almost all of their time and energy to anything *but* theology.

This book seeks the renewal of the church through the retrieval of the historic model of the pastor theologian. In doing do, the authors reject the brokerage model of ministry whereby the pastor is a kind of middle manager. In this view, "real" theology is done by guilded scholars in academic institutions, while pastors "broker" the results for their congregations. No doubt, academic theologians do have an important function in the ecology of Christian formation. But the social bifurcation between church and academy that has marked Western culture since the Enlightenment does not excuse local church pastors from one of their own major responsibilities. "Pastors are the theological chief executive officers of the church," Hiestand and Wilson boldly proclaim.

This is a gutsy book, and it raises important questions for seminaries and divinity schools as well as for those people called to lead local congregations. As one who has spent some forty years teaching in and leading institutions of theological education, I wonder how well we are doing in preparing God-called men and women to be pastor theologians in the service of the church. This book does not argue that one size fits all, for the Lord also calls ministers whose primary work is counseling, administration, evangelism, and so forth. But Hiestand and Wilson do identify the diminution of pastor theologians in our time as one of the major causes for anemic Christianity today.

I love the vision of pastors as ecclesial theologians. I would like to deepen that image in one respect, and I think the two authors would agree with me here. An ecclesial theologian must also be an ecumenical theologian—*ecumenical* in the sound, orthodox sense of that word. That means, a pastor theologian is concerned with the entire people of God through the ages and also with the *missio Dei* throughout the entire *oikoumenç* today, that is, the whole inhabited world (Luke 2:1). Such pastors honor and cherish the discrete traditions from which they come, but they also know themselves to belong to the one, holy, catholic, and apostolic church, which is the Body of Christ extended throughout time as well as space. Theology that is truly biblical and evangelical is done for, with, and in the context of this enlarged Ecclesia for which Christ died.

Timothy George, founding dean of Beeson Divinity School
of Samford University and general editor of the
Reformation Commentary on Scripture

CHAPTER 1

Pastor *or* Theologian? A Division of Labor, a Crisis of Identity

In all denominations there are pastors and priests of extraordinary intellectual ability, equally as capable of theological scholarship as academic theologians, who lack only the time, context, and encouragement for such pursuits ... on their emergence as a formative influence the renewal of the church depends.[1]   *Wallace Alston*

Pastors don't know who they are or what they are supposed to be. Perhaps no profession in the modern world suffers from a greater lack of clarity as to the basic requirements of the job. This reveals what is nothing less than a crisis of identity, which surely contributes to the high levels of burnout among pastors—and the sometimes insane attempts to conceal this burnout with various forms of self-medication, from booze to pornography to complete emotional disengagement and resignation. In the words of Princeton Seminary President M. Craig Barnes, the hardest thing about being a pastor today is "confusion about what it means to be the pastor."[2]

Identity is, of course, a trendy topic. But that doesn't mean it ought to be taboo for intelligent conversation. It's a trending topic for a reason; our world is rootless, ephemeral. Many of us, pastors not least, feel like anxious and unscripted stutterers, to borrow a phrase from Alasdair MacIntyre.[3] We've somehow lost the script that tells us who we are, what part we play, what to wear, when to come on stage, what to say, who to interact with. In the case of the pastoral vocation, this is an especially acute problem because we've lost touch with the ancient traditions of the church. What was once a readily accessible and compelling vision of the pastorate is now buried under six feet of dirt.

---

1. Quoted in Michael Welker and Cynthia A. Jarvis, *Loving God with Our Minds: The Pastor as Theologian* (Grand Rapids: Eerdmans, 2004), xiii.

2. M. Craig Barnes, *The Pastor as Minor Poet: Texts and Subtexts in Ministerial Life* (Grand Rapids: Eerdmans, 2008), 4.

3. See Alasdair MacIntyre, *After Virtue: A Study in Moral Theory*, third edition (Notre Dame: University of Notre Dame Press, 2007), 216.

Hence, this book, which is our modest attempt to help resurrect a once-thriving but now-deceased vision of the pastor, namely, the pastor theologian.

In 2006 we cofounded the Center for Pastor Theologians (CPT), an organization dedicated to assisting pastors in the study and written production of biblical and theological scholarship, for the ecclesial renewal of theology and the theological renewal of the church.[4] That's a mouthful, but what it means is this: the Center's mission is to help pastors provide intellectual leadership to the church and to the church's leaders.

The Center is pursuing a multipronged strategy to accomplish this goal. We have hosted numerous theological symposia in Chicago, sponsored two continuing study groups made up of pastors from all over the country, published an online and print journal, funded research fellowships, launched a national theology conference, and worked to capture the imagination of the next generation of pastors and theologians with the prospect of combining pastoral ministry and theological scholarship in the calling of the pastor theologian.

The pastors involved with the Center hail from a variety of church backgrounds and ecclesial traditions: Anglican, Presbyterian, Wesleyan, Messianic Jewish, Baptist, Lutheran, Pentecostal, Evangelical Free, and independent Bible church. Each has their own ecclesial convictions and characteristics, yet all are united in their agreement that theological scholarship and the pastorate belong together.

But this assumption of the CPT and its pastors is not at all common within North American evangelicalism. By and large, pastors aren't viewed as theologians, but as practitioners. As such, pastors who desire to do robust theological work for the good of the church find they're often misunderstood by both the academy and their congregations. And the result? Frustration and, not infrequently, isolation.

We recall the first gathering of our second CPT study group. After a scrumptious dinner of Chicago's finest pizza, we gathered in the living room to share highlights and, yes, lowlights from the previous year of ministry. There were a dozen relatively young pastors, all of whom had or were completing PhDs in various theological specialties. Most were meeting one another for the first time.

As they began to share about their ministries, each spoke of the tension

---

4. For more about the Center for Pastor Theologians, go to www.pastortheologians.com.

they felt between their pastoral work and their desire for theological scholarship. In fact, as we worked our way around the room, there developed a palpable sense of "me too!" Until that moment, most of these pastors felt completely alone in their efforts to bring together what seemed like two diverging worlds. One dear individual, so overwhelmed to be at last with fellow travelers, broke down and began to cry.

These study groups continue to meet each year, and we now joke that our first gathering was like a meeting of Alcoholics Anonymous—each pastor taking his turn to confess to being a pastor theologian, while the rest of us in the circle offered a sympathetic smile and nod of the head as our affirmation of support.

"Hi, I'm Todd. I'm a pastor theologian."

"Hi, Todd!"

The Pastor Theologian: A Rare Species

Pastor theologians aren't extinct, but sightings are rare. This is because pastors no longer traffic in ideas. They cast vision, manage programs, offer counsel, and give messages. We expect our pastors to be able to preach; we expect them to know how to lead; we expect them to be good at solving problems and giving direction. None of this is inherently wrong. Indeed, all of these are important pastoral tasks.

But we no longer view the pastorate as an *intellectual* calling. To be sure, we still expect pastors to know more about the Bible than your average congregant. And we usually expect pastors to know a bit of theology and apologetics to be able to speak winsomely to a student or a skeptic.

But we don't expect pastors to be *theologians*, certainly not scholars, at least not of a professional variety. Intellectually speaking, we expect pastors to function, at best, as intellectual middle management, passive conveyors of insights from theologians to laity. A little quote from Augustine here, a brief allusion to Bonhoeffer there. That's all.

This vision of the pastor as intellectual middle management is understandable, as far as it goes. A pastor ought to translate the ideas of the theological community into the language of the average Christian. But here's the rub. We no longer expect a pastor to be a bona fide, contributing member of the theological community. Sure, he may have spent a few years on the academic mountaintop, listening to the voice of the scholarly gods, before descending to his own congregation with a few choice oracles from heaven. But that heady atmosphere isn't his natural habitat; he's called to more pedestrian concerns like budgets and buildings, small groups and services, leadership meetings and pastoral visitations.

But as we will suggest in the pages to follow, this division of labor between the intellectuals and theologians, on the one hand, and the pastors as practitioners and translators, on the other, departs from historical precedent. In the not-so-distant past, and in many of the church's richest traditions, the pastorate was considered one of the most scholarly of vocations. Indeed, in pre–Civil War America, the pastorate was a go-to calling for intellectuals. If a man was unusually gifted and sought a career in which he could make full use of his mental prowess, he could hardly find a better option than the pastorate.

Think of New England pastors like Jonathan Edwards of Northampton (1703–58), Samuel Hopkins of Newport (1721–1803), Joseph Bellamy of Bethlehem (1719–90), or Nathaniel Taylor of New Haven (1786–1858). They were like their Reformation-era predecessors — "trained theologians who combined spiritual urgency with profound learning."[5] And because of this, they were able to provide first-rate intellectual leadership on all sorts of social and ecclesiastical issues — from sacramentology to soteriology, from moral reform to human rights, from theories of the atonement to the nature of the will. What is more, they were catalysts for revival and yet critiqued revival; they preached learned sermons and yet counseled the downtrodden; they wrote philosophical essays and yet weighed in on civil matters; they offered theological rationale for global missions and yet founded colleges and tutored budding theologians. Truly, they were men of whom the world is not worthy.

Interestingly, at least to us nowadays, this was an era when the term *theologian* (or *divine*) was often used synonymously with *pastor*, so overlapping were these two vocational identities within early North America. This, of course, is not to say that every seventeenth- or eighteenth-century pastor was busy producing Jonathan Edwards–like treatises, nor even that every pastor was theologically gifted to do so. But it is to say that people generally looked to pastors for theological leadership.

But how times have changed! Clearly, the academy, with its guild of professional theologians, has long since replaced the local congregation as the vocational home for theologians. We will describe some of the reasons

---

5. Richard F. Lovelace, *Dynamics of Spiritual Life: An Evangelical Theology of Renewal* (Downers Grove, Ill.: InterVarsity, 1979), 49.

for this migration in future chapters, but it is worth noting here the effect this has had on both theology and the church, namely, *theology has become ecclesially anemic*, and *the church theologically anemic*.

Anemia, for those nonmedical types, is a serious medical condition due to an insufficient supply of healthy red blood cells or hemoglobin. It results in a lack of oxygen in the body, and fatigue is one of the leading symptoms. So too the lack of pastor theologians in the church is a serious moral and spiritual condition in which there is an insufficient amount of ecclesial substance to our theology and theological substance to our churches.

The Theological Anemia of the Church, the Ecclesial Anemia of Theology

As theologians moved from churches to universities, the theological red-blood-cell count within the pastoral community, and within congregations, fell markedly. No longer is the pastoral community as a whole able to provide serious intellectual leadership for the crucial issues facing the church. Sadly, this deficiency has been further exposed—and the entire situation further exacerbated—in light of our unique post-Christian cultural moment.

The church in every age confronts new and unique challenges. But we in the twenty-first century find ourselves in an especially trying environment. The old social order (which was at least stable, if not wholly admirable), and the system of morality that accompanied it, has fractured and is now collapsing. We now confront moral choices and ethical ambiguities that did not trouble our parents' generation. Human cloning, stem cells, state sanctioned same-sex marriage, the use and limits of technology, global free-market economy, radicalized religious extremism and terrorism—all of these are enormously complex issues that require thoughtful Christian engagement if the church is going to do more than stand idly by while we watch Rome burn.

Yet the truth is that the pastoral community is not, in the main, positioned to provide strong intellectual leadership on these issues. Consequently, local churches now suffer from a sort of theological anemia not representative of our past. It should not surprise us that the near-universal removal of our theologians from the pastorate has resulted in a deep and chronic theological deficit within our congregations.

Not only has the church become *theologically* anemic, but theology has become *ecclesially* anemic. With the dawning of universities in the twelfth century, and then the onset of the Enlightenment, European intellectuals gradually ceased to view the pastoral vocation as the best context for robust intellectual engagement. The same pastoral migration we saw in Europe took place in earnest in the early nineteenth century in North America as well. With the post-Enlightenment secularization of the academy, theologians find themselves preoccupied with concerns that often only relate to the church tangentially. The result is a lot of theological heavy lifting that fails to generate much in the way of doxology or spiritual formation.

The situation is perhaps not as dire when we take into account the professors of Christian colleges, seminaries, and divinity schools. Many of them no doubt operate self-consciously as *Doctores Ecclesiae*, theologians and scholars for the church, and their vocational setting may well provide them with the intellectual freedom and institutional support they need to pursue such a calling.

But even in such settings, the methodological agnosticism that reigns within the university and its disciplines and guilds has a formative (albeit usually subtle) effect on intellectual endeavors. To put it concretely, it is not hard to spot the difference between the pastorally engaged and theologically earnest tone of, say, a Luther or Calvin or Wesley, and the disinterested, measured, and scientific posture that has become the *soup du jour* for submissions in academic journals of theology today.

To be sure, academic theology has many clear strengths; our comments are not intended to be dismissive either of it or of the academy. But we insist that since the dawning of the Enlightenment and the vacating of theologians from pastorates, theology has become increasingly professionalized and thus "academic" in ways not always relevant to the church.

A New Division of Labor

What can be done to correct this twofold problem of the theological anemia of the church and the ecclesial anemia of theology? Certainly, there is no magic cure or quick panacea. But we are convinced that, practically speaking, the problem is tied to an unhealthy division of labor that now exists between pastors and theologians. To put it simply, pastors aren't theologians, and theologians aren't pastors.

Perhaps you have heard the old yarn about the young girl who strolled with her parson father through the country church's adjacent graveyard. She liked to read the inscriptions on the headstones. This particular day, one modestly adorned tomb caught her attention. It simply had the deceased's name, dates of birth and death, and title: "Pastor Theologian." But when the girl saw those two words side-by-side on a single headstone, her face lit up with a mixture of surprise and fascination, and she declared to her father, "Papa, they have two people buried in there!"

This would be funny if it weren't so true. Of course, we need theologians, and we need pastors. But we must no longer content ourselves with the unhappy fact that these two designations ("Pastor Theologian") almost always refer to two different individuals. That has not always been the case, and we believe it should no longer be the case. In fact, we are convinced that the church needs to chart a new course. And yet the way forward will be a return to the past — the recovery or even resurrection of an ancient vision, that of the pastor theologian.

Our hope is that this book will serve as a clear call to an emerging generation of theologians to consider the pastorate as a viable vocational calling for serious theological leadership, by which we do not simply mean that pastors ought to take theology more seriously (as true as that may be). Rather, we mean that some pastors must take up the mantel of theologian by providing solid thought leadership to the church and its theologians, even as they tend the garden of their own congregations.

Of course, not every pastor is so called. But some are. Yet in the current state of affairs, serious theology or divinity students who have a love of scholarship yet a heart for the church often find themselves torn right down the middle; they perceive the division of labor that exists between pastors of local churches and theologians within the academy, and they feel forced to choose one or the other.

But there can be no turning back the clock to a more opportune time. With all of its blessings and banes, the academy is here to stay. And as we will argue in a subsequent chapter, we do not envision the pastor theologian and the academic theologian doing the same thing or needing to compete for turf; surely, there is room for a healthy division of labor between these two theologians, each one leveraging his own vocational context to the full.

But we do envision and want to advocate for a return of the pastor theologian who has a shepherd's heart and a pastor's primary vocational identity, yet who functions as an intellectual peer of the academic theologian and, as such, produces theological scholarship for the broader ecclesial community that helps shape and inform academic, cultural, and ecclesial discussions with a view to deepening the faith of the people of God. The standard division of labor, in which academics handle theological leadership and pastors deal with practical matters, is simply insufficient.

There are, of course, many challenges in counteracting this division of labor. Just as the culture of the modern university is not always sensitive to ecclesial concerns, so the culture of the contemporary congregation is hardly conducive to allowing pastors to delve into theological scholarship. There are some major concerns here, and we will make an effort to address some of them in the last section of this book. But before we tackle the pragmatic challenges of resurrecting the pastor-theologian paradigm, we must first chart a new vision for the pastor theologian, both the need and identity.

Book Overview

Understanding the legacy of the pastor theologian, and how he has functioned in the life of the church, is vital for resurrecting the paradigm. As a result, the second chapter of our book offers a sweeping historical survey of the legacy of the pastor theologian, exploring the church's historic division of labor between clerical and nonclerical theologians. As we will suggest, a main vocational home for theologians up to the mid-eighteenth century was the church, especially within the Protestant tradition.

The third chapter extends the historical narrative from the Enlightenment to the present, exploring the ways in which theologians gradually came to find a new home in the academy, largely to the exclusion of the pastorate. The contributing factors here are complex, with the European narrative and the North American narrative running in distinct (albeit, at times, parallel) directions. Whatever else might have contributed to the fading of the pastor-theologian vision, the Enlightenment in Europe and the Revolution in the Colonies played a decisive role. In this chapter, we will explore both historical events with an eye to the present context.

The fourth chapter unpacks the first of two distinct challenges facing the church due to the removal of theologians from the pastorate: the theological anemia of the church. As theologians moved away from the pastorate, the pastoral vocation came to be viewed less as a distinctly theological vocation. Over time, an unhealthy division of labor ensued, in which academics have come to be viewed as theologians and pastors have come to be viewed as practitioners. This division of labor, though well-intended, masks the inevitable reality that pastors are, whether they like it or not, the theological leaders of the church; the theological integrity of the church will never rise above its pastors, no matter how astute the local university's religion department. And insofar as pastors have largely lost their ability to provide theological leadership, and indeed no longer see doing so as part of their vocation, the theological integrity of our congregations has suffered considerably. But most significantly, as an inevitable consequence, with the collapse of theological integrity in our churches, a corresponding erosion of ethical integrity has followed.

The fifth chapter takes up the second challenge facing the church due to theology's isolation within the academy: the ecclesial anemia of theology. Not only does the church suffer from theological anemia, but theology suffers from ecclesial anemia. Key to understanding this situation is coming to terms with the reality and effect of social location on theological formation. The social location of theologians establishes the framework through which they approach the theological task. The questions asked, the answers considered, the sources consulted, the entire scholarly mode of operation—all of this is shaped by the social context of a theologian. And at the risk of stating the obvious, the social location of the academy is distinct from that of the local congregation. As such, and through no fault of their own, academic theologians tend to speak in their scholarship only tangentially to ecclesial concerns.

Chapters 6 and 7 then move us to the constructive proposal of this book: the pastor theologian as an ecclesial theologian. While a resurgence of the pastor theologian is vital to address the twofold problem already mentioned, a more precise definition of the pastor theologian is needed if real change is to take place. Toward this end, we offer in chapter 6 a taxonomy of the pastor theologian: the pastor theologian as *local theologian*, *popular theologian*, and *ecclesial theologian*. The local theologian is a pastor who provides theology to a local congregation; the popular theologian offers more widely accessible theological reflection for a broader swath of the church; and the ecclesial theologian gives theological leadership to other theologians and scholars, all the while keeping a close eye on genuine ecclesial (as opposed to academic) concerns. Fleshing out the vision of the pastor theologian as ecclesial theologian is the goal of chapter 7.

While we are convinced that all three types of pastor theologians are essential to the health of the church, our chief concern in this book is with the recovery of the ecclesial theologian. For this calling, we believe, is indispensable to the reshaping of the theological identity of the pastoral vocation. The ecclesial theologian is a return to the days when pastors wrote penetrating theological works to other theologians and churchmen, for the glory of God and the health of his people. It is this particular type of pastor theologian we are especially interested in seeing restored in the life of the church; as such, it is this particular pastor theologian that concerns the bulk of this book.

When we first began talking to others about our vision for the ecclesial theologian, the conversation invariably ran along the following lines:

Interested Person: "Oh, so you're working to resurrect theologically astute pastors" (that is, local theologians).

Us: "Yes, for sure. But we're also looking to resurrect pastors who are actively engaged in writing theology."

Interested Person: "Oh, then you mean pastors who write theology in such a way that congregants can actually understand it" (that is, popular theologians).

Us: "Sort of, but not really. We envision pastors who write theology to other intellectuals and theologians."

Interested Person (with some incredulity): "Oh, then do you mean pastors who write academic theology?" (that is, academic theologians).

Us: "No. We envision a pastor who is engaged in a kind of theological scholarship that is as intellectually robust as academic theology yet distinct from academic theology. We call it *ecclesial* theology; that is, theology that is germinated within the congregation, that presses toward distinctly ecclesial concerns, and that is cultivated by practicing clergy."

What usually follows is a quizzical look and a request for more explanation. Hence, the reason for this book. The remainder of chapter 7 attempts to delineate our vision of the ecclesial theologian vis-à-vis the academic theologian.

Chapter 8 makes an effort to move beyond theory to the nuts and bolts of our vision for the ecclesial theologian. Toward this end, we suggest ten practical steps for how one might flesh out the ecclesial-theologian paradigm in a local church context. These steps relate to education, hiring of staff, scheduling, sabbaticals, and working with a church board. As will be evident throughout the book, our vision for the ecclesial theologian runs counter to many of the currents now at work in local church ministry. As such, intentional, even institutional, steps will need to be taken to see this vision become a reality.

The final chapter of the book is a call to arms, addressed to students, pastors, and academics. Ultimately, the realization of the ecclesial-theologian vision lies with the next generation of theologians and pastors. And with this chapter, we make our best effort to convince those feeling a tug between the academy and the church to seriously consider the church as the best place to satisfy both their theological and ecclesial impulses.

Conclusion

We are under no illusions that a resurgence of the pastor theologian will rectify all the ills of the church. True Christian piety, expressed most fully and properly in love for God and neighbor, does not require intellectual sophistication; in fact, we can think of many sophisticated Christians (perhaps even a few theologians!) who remind us more of Pharisees than Christ. Let's not forget that at the final judgment God won't quiz anyone on the hypostatic union or ask anyone to explain the Trinity or expect anyone to pontificate on a proper theory of the atonement. Which is, of course, good news indeed! Because who among us can speak adequately of such things? As every honest theologian must acknowledge, the span of God's truth stretches beyond even the most brilliant of human minds. Mercifully, then, knowing the living Christ isn't precisely the same as understanding the person of Christ.

And yet the whole New Testament appears to be one sustained appeal to know the living God and his world. "Do you not *know* ... ?" the apostle Paul asks seven times in his first epistle to the Corinthians. (Because if you did, you wouldn't be doing what you're doing!) The crisis that Paul confronted in his letter to the Corinthian church was a moral crisis. But it was a moral crisis exacerbated and enabled by a crisis of *thought*. So too his letter to the Galatians. And the letter to the Hebrews. And Peter's epistles. And James' epistle. And John's first epistle. Correct understanding can't get us all the way there, but wrong understanding is often all that is needed to shipwreck one's faith. And it is the pastor's duty, above all others, to guard the theological integrity of the people of God.

We believe the vision we offer here is at once both fresh and familiar. It is fresh in that contemporary evangelicals have abandoned this vision of the pastorate. But it is familiar for all who remember the church's history.

There was a day (not too long ago) when to be a theologian was, most naturally, to be a pastor. And it is not insignificant that many (arguably most!) of the church's greatest theological leaders throughout history have been pastors.

Again, not every pastor needs to be a pastor theologian in the sense we are calling for here. The pastoral community will always need gifted leaders, visionaries, managers, counselors, and preachers, just as much as it needs gifted theologians. Yet theology is not simply another leg in the stool; rather, it is the floor upon which the legs rest. And it is this aspect of the pastoral vocation that is most neglected today by contemporary evangelicalism. Thus, it is this vision in most need of resurrection.

Above all, it is our hope that this current generation of pastors, seminarians, postgraduates, and professors will grapple with the proposal here put forth. And it is our prayer in faith that God will raise up a new generation of pastors capable of fulfilling the responsibility to which they have been called, to provide theological leadership to the church, that the church might be renewed in life and mission—for the glory of her Savior and the advance of his kingdom in this world.

CHAPTER 2

The Pastor Theologian in Historical Perspective: From the Apostolic Fathers to the Enlightenment

> Our past is sedimented in our present, and we are doomed to mis-identify ourselves, as long as we can't do justice to where we come from.[1]
>
> Charles Taylor

The British theologian and scholar N. T. (Tom) Wright is for many a consummate example of a contemporary pastor theologian. Wright graduated from Oxford University with a DPhil in New Testament and began his career in 1981 teaching New Testament at McGill University. He returned to Oxford five years later, where he taught New Testament from 1986 to 1993. But Wright left the academy in 1994 to become dean (Anglican speak for "Senior Pastor") at Lichfield Cathedral in Staffordshire, England. From there, he held various ecclesial posts until 2010, the most recent as the Bishop of Durham.

As much as any evangelical cleric in recent history, N. T. Wright has worked hard to bridge the vocational divide between the church and the academy. Wright stated his commitment to both worlds in 2004: "I think that I have been right to combine the two.... I think both the church and the academy have suffered from the disjunction. I think it's important that some people at least get to that particular place of pain, which is a place of, as it were, cultural pain. Not least in North America, maybe more in North America than England."[2]

Yet in the end, Wright's ecclesial duties were incompatible with his calling as a theologian and scholar. After sixteen years in ecclesial ministry, Wright returned to the academy in 2010, taking up a New Testament

---

1. Charles Taylor, *A Secular Age* (Cambridge, Mass.: Harvard University Press, 2007), 29.

2. N. T. Wright, "An Interview with N. T. Wright (Part 1 of 6)," *Gower Street*, interviewed by Jason Fout (November 17, 2004), http://www.gowerstreet.blogspot.com/2004/11/interview-with-nt-wright-part-1-of-6.html.

research professorship at the University of St. Andrew's in Scotland. Announcing his career move, Wright stated,

> This has been the hardest decision of my life. It has been an indescribable privilege to be Bishop of the ancient Diocese of Durham, to work with a superb team of colleagues, to take part in the work of God's kingdom here in the north-east, and to represent the region and its churches in the House of Lords and in General Synod. I have loved the people, the place, the heritage and the work. But my continuing vocation to be a writer, teacher and broadcaster, for the benefit (I hope) of the wider world and church, has been increasingly difficult to combine with the complex demands and duties of a diocesan bishop. I am very sad about this, but the choice has become increasingly clear.[3]

As Wright's example illustrates, modernity has not been kind to the pastor theologian. Attempts to live on the fault line that divides church and academy can lead, as Wright notes, to a "particular place of pain," and sometimes the pain can be unbearable. The press and pull of contemporary parish ministry does not easily lend itself to sustained theological reflection and scholarship. Beyond this, the pastor theologian finds himself in a sort of no-man's-land between two worlds, at home in neither. The laity in his congregation suspects he's wasting his time on theological mumbo jumbo that has no connection with real life, while at the same time, he is isolated vocationally and relationally from the scholarly resources of the academy.[4] The contemporary situation is, to be candid, fairly dire. Yet pastoral ministry has not always been such rocky soil for theologians.

Throughout most of the church's history, the pastoral vocation was a primary vocation for theologians and biblical scholars. One need only think of history's most important theologians to be reminded that the pastoral office was once compatible with robust theological scholarship. Irenaeus, Athanasius, Basil, Gregory of Nyssa, Gregory of Nazianzus, Augustine, Gregory the Great, Anselm, Calvin, Edwards, Wesley, etc.,

---

3. Justin Taylor, "N. T. Wright Leaving Durham, Appointed to Chair at St. Andrews," *The Gospel Coalition* (April 27, 2010), http://www.thegospelcoalition.org/blogs/justintaylor/2010/04/27/n-t-wright-leaving-durham-appointed-to-chair-at-st-andrews/.

4. An example of this can be found in the fact that pastors have no easy access—as pastors—to university library holdings, online reference works, and databases. Even divinity schools, whose primary charter is to train pastors, frequently rescind access to their library holdings upon graduation. Whatever such schools intend for their students to do upon graduation, continued scholarship while working in pastoral ministry doesn't appear to be one of them.

all demonstrate the historic and native relationship between theological leadership and the pastoral vocation.

But we have lost sight of this heritage. Our collective living memory no longer extends back to the majority narrative of the church with respect to the pastor theologian. What was once normative—theologians *as* pastors—is now novel. Given the aims of this book, and the unfortunate divorce between theological scholarship and pastoral ministry, it is time for the church to remind itself of its history—one that reveals a more amicable relationship between pastors and theologians, in which, as often as not, the two were found in one flesh.

Toward this end, we offer in this chapter a generalist account of the historic relationship between the church, the pastorate, and theological scholarship, covering five major periods of church history: Apostolic Fathers to Constantine (90–300), Constantine to the monasteries (300–600), monasteries to the universities (600–1200), universities to the Reformation (1200–1500), and the Reformation to the Enlightenment (1500–1750). In the main, the pastor theologian had a strong presence throughout the first 1,200 years of the church, with a slightly diminished yet substantial presence—especially in the Protestant tradition—until the period just before the Enlightenment. Notably, the post-Enlightenment period seems to mark the rapid decline and near extinction of the pastor theologian (the subject of chapter 3).

No single chapter—or even a single book—can do justice to the full sweep of this narrative. But the skeletal picture we offer here is, we believe, important as a context-setting framework for our subsequent discussion of the pastor theologian. In our telling of this narrative, we do not attempt a revisionist account, but rather simply do our best to present a fairly standard picture of the pastor theologian in church history. Specialists will no doubt prefer more nuance at certain points, but the overall sketch, we believe, accurately reflects the main movements of the narrative.

For the sake of clarity, and at risk of oversimplification, our chapter works with three general classifications—clerical theologians, nonclerical theologians, and monastic theologians. Arguably, all theologians up until the Enlightenment can be classified as "clerical" insofar as all theologians saw themselves as serving the church. Yet our aim in recounting the larger narrative is to highlight the extent to which theologians throughout history worked in formal ecclesial contexts and carried shepherding responsibilities for congregations and parishes (i.e., priests, pastors, bishops, etc.).

As part of our preparation for writing this narrative, we examined three major collections of theological texts: Jacques-Paul Migne's *Patrologiae Cursus Completus*, Alexander Street Press's *The Digital Library of Classic Protestant Texts*, and its twin, *The Digital Library of the Catholic Reformation*. Taken together, these three collections of theological works span nearly the whole of Western Christianity (and much of the East), up to the early eighteenth century, and include over five hundred authors. For the purposes of our survey, we analyzed the vocational contexts of the authors represented in these collections and noted the ratio of clerical theologians, monastic theologians, and nonclerical theologians for each of our five main periods. Not every text in these collections is a theological text, nor are all the texts within them written by theologians, per se. And of course, there were Christian authors not represented in these collections. Yet given the scope of these collections, the three series—taken as a whole—provide a unique perspective into the narrative of the pastor theologian. We have noted our findings for each of our five periods in the footnotes. Those interested in our full analysis of these collections may consult the appendix.

Apostolic Fathers to Constantine (90–300)

In the first century, Christian theologians, as such, were only just emerging.[5] Theological conversations tended to be pastoral and intramural, and robust interaction with pagan philosophical and religious thought was minimal. In the early stages of the church's development, persecution—more than false teachers or pagan philosophy—was the primary bane of God's people, and much early Christian writing tended to be exhortative rather than theological.[6] But as the second century unfolded, Christian intellectuals began to engage with wider Greek and Jewish thought in a more theologically proper sense. As the role of the Christian theologian matured into a full-time vocation, theologians moved toward both clerical and nonclerical vocations.[7]

---

5. Attempts to define the term *theologian* run the risk of anachronism when considered in a broad survey of this nature. Yet offering a working definition will be helpful to orient the reader. By *theologian* we have in mind a person who provides written-thought leadership for and on behalf of the Christian community regarding matters of faith, practice, apologetics, philosophy, or biblical scholarship (or some combination thereof). Here the term *written* is important, as will be seen in our later distinction between local and ecclesial theologians (the subject of chapter 6).

6. One can see this exhortative emphasis in the writings of the Apostolic Fathers, most especially Ignatius.

7. Of the twenty-one authors represented in Migne's collection during this period, thirteen were clerical writers and eight were nonclerical writers. See the appendix for more detail.

Nonclerical Theologians: 90–300

Pagan philosophers in the Greco-Roman world were often funded by wealthy patrons or supported themselves via schools formed after the manner of Plato's Academy or Aristotle's Lyceum. These two occupational patterns provided the model for many early Christian thinkers who generally viewed Christianity as the true philosophy toward which the best of pagan philosophy only gestured. Such was the case with two of the most influential nonclerical theologians of the earliest fathers—Justin Martyr and Origen.

Justin Martyr (c. 100–165), most famous of the early Christian apologists, is the earliest nonclerical theologian of whom we have any significant biographical data. Like a number of other early Christian theologians, Justin began as a pagan philosopher but became disillusioned with Platonism. After his conversion to Christianity, he continued wearing the *pallium* (the cloak of the ancient philosopher) and set up school in Rome.[8] His writings responded to both Judaism and paganism and demonstrated a learned mind capable of thinking theologically about the Christian faith. Notably, Justin's intellectual career followed the already established vocational pattern of the Greco-Roman philosophical tradition—a school formed around a master-teacher.

So also Origen (c. 184–253) of Alexandria, Egypt. Origen was raised in a devout Christian home, and Eusebius—the great fourth-century church historian—tells us that Origen's father was martyred when Origen was just sixteen years old.[9] This had a lasting effect on Origen, whose zeal for the faith was increased by this loss rather than diminished. His intellectual brilliance was obvious, and he was sought early in life as a teacher and catechizer. Though he was ordained a priest (amidst some controversy) while visiting Caesarea, the bulk of his life was spent as a philosopher and teacher. Origen traveled widely throughout the Roman Empire and was well-known for his vast erudition and theological learning. He was at various points funded by wealthy female patrons whose support allowed him to turn his lectures into books. According to Jerome, Origen wrote some two thousand treatises (other ancient sources estimate as many as six thousand),[10] and during his day, he was considered to be the leading light among Christian theologians. Despite later condemnation of his teachings

---

8. "St. Justin Martyr," in *The Oxford Dictionary of the Christian Church*, 3rd Rev. Ed., eds. F. L. Cross and E. A. Livingstone (Oxford: Oxford University Press, 2005).

9. Eusebius, *The Church History* 6.1.

10. Jerome, *Against Rufinus* 2.22.

at two fifth-century councils, many of his writings still survive, showing the influence of his work.

Clerical Theologians: 90–300

The church's clergy were also beginning to engage in robust theological work. As the church gradually assumed a more fixed institutional framework, the office of the presbyter, and then bishop, offered new vocational opportunities for Christian theologians. Two clerical theologians are noteworthy during this period: Irenaeus of Lyon and Cyprian of Carthage.[11]

Irenaeus of Lyon (c. 130–202) was a Greek bishop in the western provinces of the Roman Empire. Serving in and around the time of political revolution and religious persecution, Irenaeus was seminal in defending apostolic teaching against the many-headed hydra now known as Gnosticism. Throughout his major extant work, *Against Heresies*, Irenaeus demonstrates a remarkable capacity to engage with Platonic and Christian thought in a way that shaped Christian reflection for centuries. Beyond his theological work, Irenaeus lived up to his name (Greek for "peace") and was instrumental in building bridges of reconciliation between competing Christian communities with respect to the observance of Easter. Notably Irenaeus, whose work was influenced by Justin, did not follow his theological master into the vocation of a philosopher.[12]

Cyprian (c. 200–258), a generation later than Irenaeus, was likewise an influential bishop and theologian. Raised a pagan in Carthage, Cyprian was a lawyer known for his rhetoric and wealth before his conversion to Christianity. After his baptism, Cyprian sold his property, gave the proceeds to the poor, and devoted himself to studying the Bible and the writings of Tertullian (another North African lawyer-turned-Christian). Two years after his conversion, Cyprian was appointed Bishop of Carthage. His pontificate was disturbed by the persecution of Emperor Decius, and he was forced to flee Carthage. He was eventually martyred on September 13, 258. During his ministry, Cyprian wrote widely on ecclesiastical and soteriological matters, especially on the question of rebaptism—an issue that emerged in the context of the state persecution.[13]

---

11. Had biographical information survived, we might also include here Theophilus, Bishop of Antioch, a second-century apologist who wrote numerous tracts against the heresies of his day.

12. Scholars debate the extent to which Irenaeus was influenced by Justin. Whether Irenaeus was a personal acquaintance of Justin is lost to history. In any case, Irenaeus's theology is clearly indebted to Justin's work.

13. Akanji Israel, "Cyprian," in *The Oxford Encyclopedia of African Thought*, eds. F. Abiola Irele and Biodun Jeyifo (Oxford: Oxford University Press, 2010).

Summary: 90–300

Throughout this period, the lines between clerical and nonclerical theologians were porous—as can be seen in the case of Origen. Both clerical and nonclerical theologians saw themselves as servicing the catechetical and theological needs of the church, and both were influential in shaping the theological and pastoral direction of the church. A significant shift in vocational focus, however, occurred with the rise of Constantine and the Christianization of the empire.

Constantine to the Monasteries (300–600)

The fourth to the seventh centuries were some of the richest and most important centuries of Christian theological reflection. Most significantly, unresolved issues regarding Christology and the nature of the Godhead were given shape and settled at the councils of Nicaea (325) and Chalcedon (451). These creed-producing controversies were led (and contested) almost entirely by clerical theologians—whose theological influence during this period cannot be overstated. While the nonclerical theologian continued, a clear shift toward clerical theologians emerges.[14]

Nonclerical and Monastic Theologians: 300–600

Nonclerical and monastic theologians were active during this period, even if not in large numbers. Boethius (c. 480–524) is one such example. Boethius was a late Roman aristocrat, philosopher, and politician. Working in the neo-Platonic tradition, Boethius spent the majority of his life in quiet study and recreation, supported by his own resources, up to the time of his arrest and execution (likely for political reasons). Boethius deployed Aristotelian logic to address issues in Christian theology, and his use of Aristotle paved the way for subsequent medieval theologians to ground their own work in Aristotle.[15] Boethius' swan song, *The Consolation of Philosophy*, written in prison while awaiting execution, has proven to be an enduring work and remains a source of scholarly interest today.

It was also during this period that monastic theologians such as John

---

14. The dominance of the clerical theologian—both in numbers and influence—is clearly reflected in Migne's collection. Of the known authors in Migne's collection during this period, thirty-eight were clerical theologians, eleven were monastic theologians, and the remaining six were nonclerical.

15. Jeffrey Hause, "Boethius," in *The Oxford Encyclopedia of Ancient Greece and Rome*, ed. Michael Gagarin (Oxford: Oxford University Press, 2010).

Cassian (c. 360–435) began to emerge as theologians and scholars. Cassian founded some of the earliest monasteries in southern Gallia and wrote a number of treatises on the monastic life and Christian theology. His theological expertise and reputation was such that during the Nestorian controversy, his friend Pope Leo I asked Cassian to write a refutation of Nestorius.[16]

Clerical Theologians: 300–600

Clerical theologians were, by all accounts, predominant during this period — both in numbers and in influence. Indeed, the era from Constantine to the monasteries represents the noontide of the pastor theologian. Certainly, this was due in no small part to Constantine's Edict of Milan in 313 and the subsequent Christianization of the Roman state, both of which significantly raised the cultural clout of the church and its bishops. By the end of the fifth century, the church had sufficiently institutionalized (and the empire sufficiently Christianized) to make ecclesial service the primary vocational home for Christian intellectuals. Much could be said of erudite churchmen such as Ambrose, Bishop of Milan, whose preaching helped to convert the great Augustine; Eusebius, the Bishop of Caesarea, who produced the church's first work of history; the learned Jerome of the Latin Vulgate; the golden-tongued John Chrysostom; or the stern Cyril of Alexandria. Bishops all. Yet two sterling examples can be seen in Athanasius and Augustine.

Athanasius (c. 296–373) was the Bishop of Alexandria and one of the truly remarkable figures of church history. Beloved by his congregation, Athanasius's was no quiet life of reflection. Throughout his career, he was absorbed in the political and even economic realities of Alexandria. Most significantly, the Arian heresy was in full flower in Alexandria, and Athanasius was swept up in the political intrigue that inevitably accompanied doctrinal disputes. Remarkably, he was exiled five times from his see for his anti-Arian stance yet always found a way to return.[17] Somehow, amid the political and ecclesiastical turmoil, he managed to almost single-

---

16. David Hugh Farmer, "Cassian," in *The Oxford Dictionary of Saints*, 5th Rev. Ed. (Oxford: Oxford University Press, 2011).

17. For an exhaustive (and perhaps exhausting) treatment of Athanasius's involvement in the Arian controversy — his exiles, ecclesial intrigue, and political maneuverings — see Archibald Robertson's introduction in *Athanasius* (Nicene and Post-Nicene Fathers 2). Additionally, see Antolios, *Athanasius*, 1–38.

handedly secure the triumph of Nicaea's *homoousia* ("one substance") formula in the East. It is difficult to overstate the importance of this one bishop when it comes to the establishment of Trinitarian orthodoxy. Archibald Robertson properly remarks, "The Nicene formula found in Athanasius a mind predisposed to enter into its spirit … its victory in the East is due under God to him alone."[18]

But as influential as Athanasius was, towering above all other theologians during this time—whether clerical or nonclerical—was the great North African bishop, Augustine of Hippo (c. 354–430). Augustine's literary output was staggering. His two most famous works, *The City of God*—a lengthy defense of Christianity in the face of pagan critics—and his *Confessions*—a first-of-its-kind autobiography detailing his life and conversion (with his views on time, memory, and dreams thrown in) are just a small sampling of his larger corpus. All told, Augustine's works contain five million words.[19] It is not hyperbole to state that he wrote more than many pastors will read in a lifetime. Apart from the sheer volume of his work, his theological range was extraordinary. His writings demonstrate a profound grasp of Scripture, and he was as conversant in pagan philosophy, pagan religion, and heretical Christian teaching as he was in Christian theology. His soteriological synthesis on grace and free will, his sacramentology, his articulations of the Trinity, and, above all, his capacity for introspection still shape contemporary Christian theology. Like Athanasius, Augustine's office of bishop pulled him into the larger social and political events of his day.[20]

Summary: 300–600

During this time period, the theological legacy of pastors and bishops such as Augustine, Jerome, Athanasius, John Chrysostom, Cyril, Leo the Great, Ambrose, Hilary of Poitiers, Basil, Gregory of Nazianzus, Gregory of Nyssa, etc., far and away outstripped the achievements of the fledgling monasteries or the nonclerical theologians. Even with the full rise of the monasteries—which marks our next epoch—the dominating influence of the clerical theologian vis-à-vis the nonclerical theologian continues unabated.

---

18. *Athanasius* (Nicene and Post-Nicene Fathers 2, 4: lxix).

19. Benedict J. Groeschel, *Augustine: Major Writings* (New York: Crossroad, 1995), 1.

20. On the importance of the language of inwardness for Augustine and his impact on the rest of Western culture, see Charles Taylor, *Sources of the Self: The Making of the Modern Identity* (Cambridge: Harvard University Press, 1992), 127–42.

Monasteries to the Universities (600–1200)

A significant vocational shift takes place among theologians between the sixth and twelfth centuries, due in large measure to the monastic movement. As Christianity became increasingly wedded to—and in some ways compromised by—the political power of the day, the threat of persecution and martyrdom subsided. Health and prosperity became the new bane of the church. This gave rise to an emphasis on ascetic practices and helped fuel the monastic movement. As the monastic movement grew, new opportunities emerged for scholars to create dense networks of mutual support within the monastic communities.[21]

Nonclerical and Monastic Theologians: 600–1200

The monastic movement can be traced back to Egyptian Christianity in the third century, but the movement takes full shape in the West in the sixth century. Following the examples of the earlier monastics, many Christians began to retreat from the wider culture. Both the church and the monasteries saw the monasteries as extensions of the church and an aid to the church's mission. Many moving toward the newly founded monasteries sought a life of simplicity, contemplation, and prayer. Yet many sought a context for study and theological reflection. Medieval historian Charles Haskins notes that throughout this era, particularly toward its close, theological learning increasingly organized itself around monastic and cathedral schools.[22] Given the high cost of producing texts before the printing press, the fiduciary cooperation of the monasteries made the scholarly task possible in ways that were not possible for unfunded individual scholars.

Among the early monastics, Benedict (c. 480–550) was the most important. His life and work did more to establish the monastic tradition in the West than any other factor. Benedict was born at Nursia and studied at Rome. Dissatisfied at Rome, he left before completing his studies to become a hermit. After a number of stops along the way, he attracted to himself a band of disciples and established a monastic community at

---

21. Migne's collection during this time shows a clear growth of the monastic theologian, a reduction of the nonclerical theologian, and a yet prominent place for the clerical theologian. Of the 117 authors listed by Migne during this period, fifty-three are clerical theologians, thirty-eight are monastic theologians, and twenty-six are nonclerical theologians.

22. Charles Haskins, *The Rise of Universities* (Ithaca, N.Y.: Cornell University Press, 1957), 28–29.

Monte Cassino. There, he completed his famous *Rule of Saint Benedict*— written as a guide for the monastic life. Though little is known about his life, his *Rule* provided a framework for future generations of monks. Based on his limited extant work, it does not appear that Benedict himself was a highly productive theologian. But his leadership helped create a structure of institutional support for the emerging monastic movement.[23]

Other noteworthy monastic theologians include the Venerable Bede (c. 673–735) and John of Damascus (c. 675–749)—both influential in their day and beyond. But nonclerical theologians, on the whole, seem to have less of a reach during this time. Migne's collection presents us with figures that will be foreign to most. Names like John Malalas, a sixth-century civil servant; Hrotsvitha of Gandersheim, a tenth-century poet; and Joannes Cinnamus, a twelfth-century Byzantine historian.

Clerical Theologians: 600–1200

Even with the rise of the monastery, the bishop's office still attracted large numbers of intellectuals and theologians. Bookending this period are two notable examples—Gregory the Great and Anselm of Canterbury—both of whom began as monastic theologians.

Gregory the Great (c. 540–604), born to an aristocratic family, began his life in public service. In 573, he sold his property and founded six monasteries in Sicily, and a seventh monastery in Rome. Intending to be a monk, he entered one of his own monasteries but was eventually called out of monastic life by Pope Benedict I to serve at Rome. He hoped to lead a missionary expedition to the Anglo-Saxons but was elected pope during an outbreak of the plague. Gregory proved to be an able administrator, as can be seen in his continued missionary commitment to the Anglo-Saxons. Recruiting others to go in his stead, Gregory gave leadership to the missionary efforts that led to the conversion of the Anglo-Saxons. Beyond his administrative and missionary prowess, Gregory (after whom the Gregorian chant is named) was highly instrumental in shaping the Roman liturgy. All the while, Gregory wrote. Among his voluminous writings, he produced a harmony of the gospels and a *Moralia* on the book of Job; his work *Pastoral Care* significantly shaped clerical self-understanding throughout the Middle Ages; and his *Lives of the Saints* did much to shape the spiritual and supernatural imaginations of Christians in his generation

---

23. For an executive summary of Benedict's life and *Rule*, see Farmer, "Benedict," in *The Oxford Dictionary of the Saints*.

and the next. Beyond his formal treatises, Gregory's many letters reveal an expansive theological mind devoted to the care, administration, and theological leadership of the church.[24]

On the far end of this period, we find Anselm, Archbishop of Canterbury (c. 1033–1109), who, like Gregory, began vocationally as a monk. Anselm entered the monastery at Bec in Normandy and took his vows in 1060. Three years later, upon the death of the prior, he took over as head of the monastery. Anselm wrote much during his monastic tenure, and he gathered a reputation as a brilliant thinker and theologian. But in 1093, at the request of King William II, Anselm reluctantly agreed to become Archbishop of Canterbury. His bishopric was fraught with political strife over land disputes, and he was eventually exiled from England. But even amid the controversy and exile, Anselm continued to write. His *On the Incarnation of the Word* was completed in 1095, and his most important work, *Why God Became Man*, was finished in 1098. This later work rejected the earlier ransom theories of some of the Eastern Fathers (Origen and Gregory of Nyssa) and was influential in shaping Reformational views of the atonement and, as a consequence, still shapes Protestant thought today. His many letters written during his bishopric reveal a Christian theologian thoroughly engrossed in ecclesiastical affairs.[25] Arguably, Anselm was the most important theologian between Augustine and Aquinas.

Summary: 600–1200

The examples of Gregory and Anselm underscore the interrelatedness of the monasteries and the pastoral vocation. Strict categorization between monastic and clerical theologians is difficult. But it is clear that ecclesial service was a viable vocational path for theologians during this period— most especially the office of bishop. A change takes place, however, with the rise of the universities.

Universities to the Reformation (1200–1500)

The universities emerged at the close of the twelfth century as the new centers of learning. The early universities were not institutions as we conceive of today but rather first appeared as *universitas magistrorum et scholarium*—corporations of students and teachers—which allowed

---

24. Farmer, "Gregory the Great," in *The Oxford Dictionary of the Saints*.
25. "St. Anselm," in *The Oxford Dictionary of the Christian Church*.

students to leverage their collective identity and negotiate with the teachers key aspects of their education such as curricula, length of classes, and fee structures.[26] These corporations gradually evolved into more formal institutions, consisting of colleges and "nations" (groupings of students based on their national identity for the sake of mutual support and protection from local magistrates).[27] Among the first universities were Bologna and Paris, followed by Oxford and Cambridge. Study gradually grew to consist of four faculties: medicine, law, philosophy, and theology — with canon law and theology given precedence in the early years. The rise of the universities marks the first time the pastoral office begins to be eclipsed as the majority vocational home of theologians.

Nonclerical Theologians: 1200–1500

Before the universities, learning had centered around monastic and cathedral schools;[28] bishops, monks, and clergy did most of the heavy theological lifting. But university masters — though at first lacking professional gravitas — gained increasing prestige and status as the universities evolved into stable institutions. By the middle of the thirteenth century, those seeking theological training could not do better than to study at a prestigious university under a renowned master. With the advent and growth of the universities, the notable theologians during this period were schoolmen such as the *Doctor Subtilis*, John Duns Scotus (c. 1266–1308), and the nominalist William Ockham (c. 1287–1347), considered two of the most important theologians of the Middle Ages. And head of class among the university masters was the Dominican scholar and Paris professor, Thomas Aquinas (c. 1224–74).

Aquinas, as much as any other medieval thinker, fully exemplifies the scholastic theologian of the thirteenth to fifteenth centuries. Aquinas was born of noble stock and studied first in Naples at the Benedictine Abbey of Monte Cassino. He moved from there to the University of Naples, where he joined the Dominicans — a monastic order devoted to preaching. For

---

26. See Walter Rüegg, "Themes," in *A History of the University in Europe: Vol. 1, Universities in the Middle Ages*, ed. H. De Ridder-Symoens (Cambridge: Cambridge University Press, 1992), 20.

27. For an executive summary of the formation of the earliest universities, see Kathryn Olesko, "University," in *The Oxford Companion to the History of Modern Science*, ed. J. L. Heilbron (Oxford: Oxford University Press, 2003). For a detailed account see De Ridders-Symoens, ed., *A History of the University in Europe: Vol. 1*. See also Haskins, *Rise of Universities*.

28. Haskins lists the most influential cathedral schools as Liege, Rheims, Laon, Paris, Orleans, and Chartres. See his *Rise of Universities*, 12–13.

his theology curriculum, he went to Paris, the center of theology in the Middle Ages, and after Paris to the *studium generale* of the Dominicans in Cologne, where he studied under Albert the Great—himself no mean theologian. Aquinas completed his theological studies at the University of Paris, where he occupied a chair of theology from 1256 to 1259. Over the next ten years he taught in the Italian cities of Orvieto, Rome, and Viterbo. In 1269, he was asked to return to Paris as a professor, an indication of Thomas's high theological reputation.

Thomas's corpus is vast. The critical edition of his works is the "Leonine" edition, which began in 1882 but has yet to be completed. All told, it will contain more than fifty volumes. Thomas wrote widely on various theological subjects. His *Summa contra Gentiles* explores the relationship between divine and general revelation and was an effort to establish the intellectual coherence of the Catholic faith to skeptics. In particular, Aquinas helped to pioneer the church's appropriation of Aristotle, whose writings were only then beginning to make their way into the Latin West. His famous *Summa Theologiae* is characteristic of the disputational theology popular in his day and is still a massive shaper of Christian—and especially Catholic—theology. Thomas ranks near the top (bested perhaps only by Augustine) on a short list of the most important intellectuals of the Christian tradition.[29]

Clerical Theologians: 1200–1500

The movement of theologians toward the universities was neither immediate nor absolute; throughout this period, the clerical office—especially the bishop's office—retained a significant role in shaping the church's theology. Influential bishop theologians such as Stephen Tempier (Paris, d. 1279) and Robert Kilwardby (Canterbury, c. 1215–79), as well as cardinal theologians such as Thomas Cajetan (1469–1534) in many ways exercised more theological leadership within the church than did the university masters. Tempier famously (or perhaps infamously) issued a series of condemnations directed at the University of Paris because some of the faculty were perceived to hold theological positions he considered problematic (many of his condemnations were aimed at Aquinas). So too Kilwardby issued a series of condemnations on thirty-nine positions held at Oxford (again, targeting Thomistic positions). In both instances, the condemnations of

---

29. Jan A. Aertsen, "St. Thomas Aquinas," in *The Oxford Dictionary of the Middle Ages*, ed. Robert E. Bjork (Oxford: Oxford University Press, 2010).

the bishops were not without effect, and the universities were compelled to adjust accordingly (amid controversy). And Cajetan's disputation with Luther at the Diet of Augsburg, while perhaps not warming Protestant hearts, nonetheless illustrates the theological leadership and influence of the clergy in the Middle Ages.[30]

Ecclesiastical leaders like Tempier, Kilwardby, and Cajetan were not merely heavy-handed church officials — issuing theological judgments about which they knew little. Cajetan was an established theologian in his own right, publishing a four-part commentary on Thomas's *Summa Theologiae* as well as a series of shorter works on ethical and theological topics. Kilwardby was likewise an active scholar. He produced a commentary on Peter Lombard's *Sentences* as well as numerous treatises on time, imagination, relation, and conscience, and his *De ortu scientiarum* was an important Aristotelian classification of knowledge. Kilwardby also organized large-scale indexes of patristic writings, mainly those of Augustine.[31]

Likewise, the career trajectory of the university masters and doctors indicates the continued theological prestige of the church during this period; not only did university *graduates* move toward the churches, but so also the university *professors*. During the thirteenth to fifteenth centuries, many bishops (and even some cardinals and popes) had taught in the universities, and the masters and doctors in the schools — especially those who taught canon law or theology — frequently sought high posts within the church (or were recruited to these posts by popes). To this point, historian Jacques Verger notes, "In the thirteenth century, over thirty-three percent of the recorded Parisian masters of theology became bishops, abbots, general ministers, or cardinals. In the fifteenth century, thirty-six of the seventy-nine English bishops (forty-six percent) had taught at Oxford or at Cambridge."[32] Likewise, during the fifteenth century in England, thirty-six bishops (of seventy-three) had served as chancellor, head of a college, university proctor, or in some other official position at Oxford or Cambridge.[33] There are many examples of professors who moved from the

---

30. The theological control of the bishops and popes over the universities remained largely intact until the Western Schism (1378) associated with the Avignon Papacy. With the fracturing of ecclesiastical power, the universities (especially Paris) asserted themselves as the guardians of theological orthodoxy.

31. "Kilwardby, Robert," in *The Oxford Dictionary of the Christian Church*.

32. Jacques Verger, "Teachers," in *A History of the University in Europe: Vol. 1*, 150. This is not exclusively theology, they would likely have taught law as well.

33. Joel Thomas Rosenthal, "The Training of an Elite Group: English Bishops in the Fifteenth Century," in *Transactions of the American Philosophical Society*, vol. 60.5 (1970): 17.

universities to ecclesiastical appointment in the church, but fewer examples of high-church officials (such as bishops and cardinals) moving toward the universities. This general career trajectory suggests that the ecclesial office still retained a high measure of theological gravitas and prestige vis-à-vis the universities.

The continuing import of the clerical theologian throughout this period is due, at least in part, to the fact that in important ways both the church and the universities themselves viewed the first universities as an extension of the church's mission. Until the Reformation, universities were chartered by ecclesiastical authorities to further the mission of the church and to supply the church with canon lawyers and learned clergy.[34] And many university masters—like Thomas Aquinas—were priests who were at the same time part of a monastic order. (It was eventually required that anyone holding the degree of master must be under holy orders).

Likewise, the merging together of the monastic and cathedral schools into the universities blurred the lines between church, monastery, and university. Service in the priesthood did not require a university degree, but increasingly, the higher offices within the church came to be held by university graduates. Medievalist Peter Moraw notes that from 1380 to 1500 at New College, Oxford, fifty-one percent of graduates went into some form of ecclesial ministry, with only two-and-a-half percent serving in posts exclusively in the lay world (with forty-two percent classified as "unclarified" or "early death").[35]

So too by the fifteenth century in England, a university education was all but necessary for those aspiring to the bishop's office, even more important than a high station at birth.[36] The net effect was that the university, though having its own identity, was not viewed as completely independent from the church, but rather as an extension of the church (perhaps initially not unlike how the monastic orders were viewed).[37]

---

34. Until the Reformation, universities were typically chartered by ecclesiastical authorities—popes and bishops. See Olesko, "University," in *The Oxford Companion to the History of Modern Science.*

35. Peter Moraw, "Careers and Graduates," in *A History of the University in Europe: Vol. 1*, 269. This general career trend is well illustrated by Benedict XII (c. 1280–1342) who began as monk, was eventually made abbot of his monastery, studied at Paris, was awarded the degree of master, and was appointed Bishop of Palmiers, then cardinal, and finally pope.

36. Rosenthal, "Training," 12.

37. See George Marsden, *The Soul of the American University: From Protestant Establishment to Established Nonbelief* (Oxford: Oxford University Press, 1994), 34.

Summary: 1200–1500

With respect to import of clerical theologians, the rise of the university cut both ways. Initially, the university had a positive impact on the theological integrity of the clerical office. Overall, literacy among the clergy rose, and theological education increased.[38] Yet the maturing of the university meant that the bishop's office was no longer the primary vocation of the theologian. While clerical theologians involved themselves in the disputations and happenings of the universities, the universities increasingly became the headwaters of theological production.[39] The rise of the universities, however, did not mark the absolute demise of the clerical theologian. The bishop's office continued to be the vocational home for many able scholars and theologians, and many priests who served near universities and cathedrals likewise engaged in theological scholarship.[40]

The Reformation to the Enlightenment (1500–1750)

The Reformation split the Western church into two traditions, each of which has had its own unique trajectory regarding the clerical theologian. The events of the Reformation appear to have had little effect on the vocational context of Catholic theologians. But the Reformation seems to have funneled Protestant theologians away from the universities and back into the churches in a way that represented a reversal of the previous era. During the two hundred years following the Reformation, clerical theologians within Protestantism emerge as a robust body of leading theologians, every bit the intellectual and theological equals of their university

---

38. "The generally high level of education now served to blunt the bifurcation between scholars and the other bishops, for they were almost all university graduates.... Almost all bishops now came to their sees, if not as scholars, at least as competent, well trained academics." Rosenthal, "Training," 18.

39. Rosenthal observes, "The bishops cut a rather narrow swathe in fifteenth-century thought, and they certainly did not intellectually dominate the church." See "Training," 15.

40. This contradicts the comments of Pope Benedict XVI in his *The Nature and Mission of Theology: Essays to Orient Theology in Today's Debate* (San Francisco: Ignatius Press, 1995), 115–16, when he writes, "At the close of the twelfth century theology rushed as impetuously as a flash flood from its traditional centers—the bishop's residence, the monastery and the chapter of the canons regular—to a new, ecclesiastically neutral center, the university." While it is certainly true that theologians moved into the newly established universities, such centers were not "ecclesiastically neutral"; likewise, Benedict's comment that theology "rushed as impetuously as a flash flood" into the universities is overstated and does not account for the continuing presence of vital clerical theologians.

counterparts. Insofar as our primary concern is the pastor theologian in the Protestant tradition, we here limit our discussion to the Protestant narrative.[41]

Protestant Nonclerical Theologians: 1500 – 1750

Nonclerical theologians were significant shapers of the Reformation tradition. Philipp Melanchthon (1497 – 1560) was a Wittenberg professor and an important systematizer of Luther's works; Martin Bucer (1491 – 1551) was a Dominican friar turned reformer who served as an influential ecclesiastical advisor throughout southwest Germany, and then later as a professor at Cambridge; William Tyndale (c. 1494 – 1536), a client of wealthy patrons, translated the Bible into the common vernacular; and George Fox (1624 – 91) was an influential (if controversial) antiestablishment Quaker lay preacher. And, above all, was Martin Luther (1483 – 1546) — the preeminent theologian of the Reformation.

Luther's influence can scarcely be overstated. His writings (along with the writings of Catholic humanist, Erasmus) were a chief catalyst in stirring the ecclesiastical and theological imaginations of sixteenth-century Europe. Luther began as an Augustinian monk at the Erfurt monastery in Germany and was later transferred to the monastery at Wittenberg. Luther moved rapidly through his theological studies and was awarded the doctorate in theology in 1512, whereupon he reluctantly accepted the professorship in Bible. Yet throughout this time, Luther was preoccupied by concerns regarding the state of his soul. His internal struggle to find a gracious God led ultimately to a reformulation of Christian soteriology that sparked the Reformation. Luther's subsequent conflict with the ecclesiastical authorities involved him in disputations, ecclesiastical trials, official papal condemnations of his person and views, and finally exile. Ultimately, Luther was provided safe haven in Wittenberg, where he continued as professor of Bible, leader of the German Reformation, and founder of Lutheranism.

Luther's work as a professor was the shaping theological influence of the Reformation. Yet Luther was no ivory-tower theologian. While not the pastor of the town church in Wittenberg (a position occupied by his friend Johannes Bugenhagen), Luther's involvement in ecclesial life

---

41. An examination of *The Digital Library of Classic Protestant Texts* reveals that fifty-one percent of the approximately two hundred authors in the collection were clerical theologians, while forty-nine percent were nonclerical.

was remarkable. He regularly participated in ecclesial disputes, pastoral training, and was a frequent preacher at the town church. Between 1510 and 1546, Luther preached approximately 3,000 sermons to the laity—a preaching schedule more rigorous than most contemporary pastors. As was common in Protestant pre-Enlightenment Europe, the worlds of the academy and the church merged together in ways that did not allow for easy separation. As such, Luther's writing demonstrates a deep acquaintance with the needs of average Christians.[42]

Protestant Clerical Theologians: 1500–1750

The pastoral community also brought high-level theological leadership to the Protestant cause. Examples of significant and influential clerical theologians abound. Ulrich Zwingli (1484–1531) was a Catholic priest turned Protestant pastor in Zurich, and a chief father of the Reformed tradition; Johannes Bugenhagen (1485–1558), though overshadowed by the great Luther, was the pastor at Wittenberg, an able church administrator, and a significant theologian in his own right; Thomas Cranmer (1489–1556) was the Archbishop of Canterbury and the founding father of the English Protestant church; Jacob Arminius (1560–1609), a theological opponent of Calvin, was a pastor in Amsterdam and founder of the theological system that still bears his name; John Owen (1616–83) was a renowned preacher and pastor (and later vice chancellor at Oxford) whose works are still read today. And preeminent among the clerical theologians of the Reformation was, of course, John Calvin (1509–64).

Calvin came of age as the Reformation was getting under way. Initially dedicated to the study of law in Orleans, Calvin's first love was the classics. But soon, his reading of Luther and his acquaintance with French reformers shifted his intellectual attention away from Seneca and toward the Bible. Calvin's association with Nicolas Cop—friend and rector at the University of Paris—resulted in Calvin fleeing France when Cop was brought up on heresy charges for having Lutheran views. Calvin landed in Basel and from there intended to go to Strasbourg, where he hoped to adopt the quiet life of a scholar. But a war between Charles V and Francis I interrupted his travels and resulted in an unintended layover in Geneva,

---

42. For a concise treatment of Luther's pastoral duties at Wittenberg and beyond, see John Piper, *The Legacy of Sovereign Joy: God's Triumphant Grace in the Lives of Augustine, Luther, and Calvin* (Wheaton, IL: Crossway, 2000), 86–90. See also, Fred W. Meuser, *Luther the Preacher* (Minneapolis: Augsburg, 1983).

where he was compelled by the earnest admonitions of William Farel to assist in the reform of Geneva. Calvin reluctantly agreed. Their attempted reforms soon put them at odds with the town council, and Calvin was expelled from the city. Yet after three years in Strasbourg (where Calvin hoped to once again settle into the quiet life of a scholar), Calvin was recalled to Geneva by the council. He returned and this time stayed for the remainder of his life, serving as Geneva's leading pastor and theological authority.[43]

Calvin's theological output was significant. Beyond his *Institutes of the Christian Religion* (his magnum opus), he wrote numerous tracts, as well as commentaries on nearly every book of the Bible. Calvin's influence stretched beyond Geneva across Europe, and he was considered a leading theologian by those sympathetic to the Reformation. Luther spoke highly of him, and even Jacob Arminius, his theological opponent on the matter of predestination, said of Calvin, "Next to the study of the Scriptures which I earnestly inculcate, I exhort my pupils to peruse Calvin's *Commentaries*, which I extol in loftier terms than Helmich [a Dutch divine] himself; for I affirm that he excels beyond comparison in the interpretation of Scripture, and that his commentaries ought to be more highly valued than all that is handed down to us by the library of the fathers."[44]

Summary: 1500–1750

The examples of Calvin and Luther highlight the import of both clerical and nonclerical theologians in Protestantism during the sixteenth and seventeenth centuries. And the composition of Alexander Street Press's *Digital Library of Classic Protestant Texts* illustrates the dynamic and mutually supportive roles of clerical and nonclerical theologians: when taken as a whole, there is a near-even split between clerical and nonclerical authors represented in the collection (with a slight advantage to clerical theologians). Insofar as the Alexander Street Press collection represents a fair cross section of the Protestant tradition in the sixteenth and seventeenth

---

43. For an executive summary of Calvin's career and theology, see Alexandre Ganoczy, "Calvin, John" in *The Oxford Encyclopedia of the Reformation*, ed. Hans J. Hillerbrand (Oxford: Oxford University Press, 1996). For a look at John Calvin as pastor and preacher, see Scott M. Manetsch, *Calvin's Company of Pastors: Pastoral Care and the Emerging Reformed Church, 1536–1609* (Oxford: Oxford University Press, 2012). Also Piper, "The Divine Majesty of the Word," in *The Legacy of Sovereign Joy*, 115–42.

44. Philip Schaff, *History of the Christian Church*, 8 vols. (Grand Rapids: Eerdmans, 1952–53), 8:280.

centuries, clearly the pastoral office was considered a viable vocation for theologians during the Reformation and post-Reformation eras.[45]

Conclusion

The pastor theologian has had a robust and storied place in the history of God's people. Of course, not every pastor—or even most—throughout the time frame covered in our survey embraced the role of a theologian. Throughout much of the church's history, especially during the Middle Ages, not all pastors were even literate. And given the high costs of copying and preserving texts, the hard reality of economics made it prohibitive for the vast majority of parish priests to engage in scholarship. Nevertheless, the pastoral community, especially the bishops, self-consciously assumed the mantle of the church's theological leadership throughout much of the first eighteen centuries of the church. While not every pastor was a theologian, many (many!) theologians were pastors.

But times have changed. The pastoral vocation is no longer considered a viable vocation for theologians. The reasons for this change are complex, and the factors on the Continent and in Britain were different than the factors in North America. Yet in both instances, the results were the same. It is to this great divorce in the intellectual life of the church that our story now turns.

---

45. The Catholic tradition, however, seems to move along a different trajectory. In *The Digital Library of the Catholic Reformation*, the number of nonclerical authors exceeds that of clerical theologians: fifty-one percent were nonclerical theologians, thirty percent were clerical theologians, and nineteen percent were monastic theologians. Taken together, in both the Catholic and Protestant tradition, fifty percent of the theologians represented in the two Alexander Street Press collections were nonclerical theologians, forty-two percent were clerical theologians, and eight percent were monastic theologians.

CHAPTER 3

The Great Divorce:
The Demise of the Pastor Theologian
in Europe and North America

In the nineteenth century, there were two kinds of universities: German
universities and those that wanted to be German.[1]

Michael Legaspi

As late as 1776, Adam Smith wrote, "There is scarce, perhaps, to be found
anywhere in Europe, a more learned, decent, independent, and respectable
set of men, than the greater part of the Presbyterian clergy of Holland,
Geneva, Switzerland, and Scotland."[2] High praise indeed for European
clergy. But by the end of the eighteenth century, clergy were not generally
held in such high regard. Somewhere between the middle of the eighteenth
century and the present, the pastor theologian had (to quote Eusebius)
"paid nature's debt."

The European narrative and the North American narrative run along
a similar trajectory. The factors that led to the demise of the pastor theologian, however, are unique to each context. In Europe, the Enlightenment
was the decisive event. In North America, the Revolution and the Second
Great Awakening played the crucial role. In this chapter, we offer a preliminary account of both contexts, with a view to highlighting the contributing factors that led to the tragic divorce between the theologian and
the pastor. What was once viewed as a single occupation came to be seen
as two distinct—and mutually exclusive—vocations.

---

1. Michael Legaspi, *The Death of Scripture and the Rise of Biblical Studies* (Oxford: Oxford
University Press, 2010), 28.
2. Adam Smith, *The Wealth of Nations*, ed. Edwin Cannan (London: Methuen, 1904),
1.1.226.

The Great Divorce in Europe

Any account of the Western intellectual tradition must pass through the upheaval of the Enlightenment. And so too must any account of the pastor theologian.

The Enlightenment was birthed in the wake of the "new science" of Galileo and Newton. New discoveries, particularly in physics and planetary motion, brought about the demise of the Aristotelian metaphysics to which medieval Christianity had been wed. The old saying was proved true: the one who marries the spirit of the age is destined to be a widower.

As Aristotle fell like Newton's apple, the church's theologians found themselves searching for a new place to stand. The "Galileo Affair" has been overdrawn, as has the church's conflict with science in the eighteenth century. Yet it is certainly true that the church and its theologians initially found it difficult to adjust to the new scientific theories at play.

These new theories, along with the volatile cultural and political situation in France and the rest of Europe, led to devastating and sustained critiques against the church by the French *philosophes* such as Voltaire, Jean-Jacques Rousseau, and Denis Diderot—a group of anticlerical philosophers, writers, and scholars.[3] The contempt with which the *philosophes* held the institutional church—especially the Roman church—was palpable. A ready example can be found in the fact that Diderot's famous seventeen-volume *Encyclopédie*, with contributions from 160 authors and over 100 consultants, and which claimed to preserve all human learning up until that time, did not contain an entry for Jesus Christ. The omission was intentional.

The church responded to the attacks of critics like Diderot and Voltaire with censorship. But the more the church suppressed its critics, the more gleefully they were received by the wider culture. The withering attacks on organized religion by the *philosophes* ignited a cultural war between clerical theologians and nonclerical philosophers in which both sides vied for the intellectual supremacy of Europe. By all accounts, the church lost.

As the smoke cleared, the church emerged intact but diminished in cultural influence. Seemingly unanswerable questions about the church's

---

3. Dan Edelstein argues persuasively that the Enlightenment was a fundamentally French movement, with effects in wider Europe. See his *The Enlightenment: A Genealogy* (Chicago: University of Chicago Press, 2010). For a detailed account of the intellectual warfare between the French *philosophes* and the church, see Alan Charles Kors, "Philosophes," in *The Encyclopedia of the Enlightenment*, ed. Alan Charles Kors (Oxford: Oxford University Press, 2002).

intellectual integrity had been raised, and it was no longer universally viewed—by intellectuals or the larger European culture—as the obvious intellectual center of Western culture. An enormous amount of optimism (which would later die in the trenches of World War I) was born regarding the ability of humanity to solve its ills through the new science and the elimination of religious censorship. The church, it was generally agreed, was part of the problem, not part of the solution.

Notably, the Enlightenment was not a product of the university or primarily a university event. Most of the *philosophes*, though they passed through the universities (with the noteworthy exceptions of Voltaire and Rousseau), were employed by sympathetic political magistrates.[4] The important conversations of the day took place in salons, clubs, and coffeehouses—not university lecture halls. Insofar as the universities still retained their Christian moorings and ties to organized religion, the Enlightenment marginalized the universities as much as it did the church. Historian Notker Hammerstein remarks, "In France in the eighteenth century, the university ceased to have any marked influence on the intellectual life of French society and the course of enlightened discussion there."[5]

Over the span of the eighteenth and nineteenth centuries, the universities, which had been largely conceived and reared in service to the churches, gradually became instruments of the state. The University of Paris, for example, came to an end with the French Revolution and was reinstituted as the University of France in 1793. This enabled the universities to regain some of their former cultural relevancy but at the cost of their original ecclesial commitments.

The effect of the Enlightenment on Christian theology cannot be overstated. The Enlightenment reshaped the scholarly and cultural consensus regarding the ontology of the Bible and the place of theology within the wider culture. The English deists, the French *philosophes*, and other radical Enlightenment thinkers generally despised or minimized the Bible. In the wake of the Enlightenment, the Bible was no longer a sacred text and theology was no longer the queen of the sciences.

---

4. Edelstein, *Enlightenment*, 90.

5. Notker Hammerstein, "Epilogue: The Enlightenment" in *A History of the University in Europe: Universities in Early Modern Europe (1500–1800), Vol. 2*, ed. Hilde De Ridder-Symoens (Cambridge: Cambridge University Press, 1996), 631. But see Edelstein, *Enlightenment*, 87, who, while acknowledging that "the universities did not belong to the avant-garde of the 'new philosophy,'" nonetheless argues for more university influence than Hammerstein allows.

The study of Scripture and theology within the universities risked dying altogether, had both subject matters not been repositioned within the German universities during the eighteenth century. The Germans, rather than dismissing the Bible, transformed the study of the Bible into an academic discipline—a precise textual science.[6] The scholarly tools used to study the classical texts of antiquity were now deployed on the Bible. Source criticism and textual criticism emerged as disciplines that sought to understand the Bible as an ancient document composed of multiple authors. The Bible's divine authorship, if acknowledged at all, faded to the background. True, German intellectuals argued, the Bible could no longer be viewed as a book of divinely revealed truth; yet it remained a culturally important artifact—as worthy of study as Homer's *Iliad* or Herodotus's *The Histories* and useful for establishing a cultural moral framework.

This German approach to Scripture became a normative approach for intellectuals throughout the Continent. Similar approaches were adopted regarding church history and theology. Modern notions of objectivity and neutrality were born and prized as methodological avenues to true scholarship. Ultimately, an academic view of Scripture eclipsed an ecclesial view of Scripture; the study of the Bible and theology within the university context has never been the same.[7]

As the nineteenth century unfolded, the intellectual credibility of the faith had been roundly and universally chastised in the West; study of the Bible and theology survived in the academy but in a radically different form. This overall repositioning of Scripture and theology within the universities was clearly not compatible with the sorts of traditional approaches that had once been useful for clergy. The resulting gap between the academy and the church became such that the German biblical studies scholar Johann David Michaelis could say in the late eighteenth century, "The academic lecture and the sermon are so different that, if done well, they will in time only corrupt one another."[8]

The Enlightenment assault on Christian belief influenced theologians within the churches as well. Presumably, the church still provided institutional space and support for Christian theologians and scholars during and after the Enlightenment. But in the wake of the Enlightenment, European

---

6. Legaspi tells this story well in his *The Death of Scripture and the Rise of Biblical Studies*.

7. For more here, see Edward Farely, *Theologia: The Fragmentation and Unity of Theological Education* (Eugene: Wipf & Stock, 1994), 39–48.

8. As quoted in Legaspi, *The Death of Scripture and the Rise of Biblical Studies*, 27.

intellectuals no longer gravitated toward the pastorate as an obvious vocational context for serious theological engagement. From the nineteenth century to the present, the (now largely) secular university eclipsed the church as the place of cultural and intellectual prestige, and intellectuals in Europe responded accordingly.

The Great Divorce in North America[9]

The North American context reflects the same general movement away from clerical theologians that we see in Europe.[10] But unlike in Europe, the decisive factor for North America was not an aggressively secular Enlightenment, but rather the American Revolution and its religious aftermath—the Second Great Awakening.

In the middle of the seventeenth century, the North American academy was only beginning to take shape. As such, it did not yet constitute a strong presence in the colonies. Consequently, the main vocational context for colonial theologians was the local church. This remained the case throughout the eighteenth century. During this time, theology in North America was advanced by pastors such as Jonathan Edwards (1703–58), Samuel Hopkins (1721–1803), and Joseph Bellamy (1719–90). Men such as these not only served as pastors to local congregations but also represented the intellectual and theological elites of their day. It was nearly always the case that the pastor was the most learned man in town. In a culture where church attendance was often mandatory—and where pastors shepherded whole towns (usually without competition)—a pastor's influence over secular and civil life was significant. This social influence translated into theological influence, both with the laity and, most notably, with the early colleges.

Unlike the present day, the theological colleges were established by local church pastors to feed the needs of local church ministry and were in large measure under the formal theological authority of the pastoral community.[11] Often, it was young men in their later teens and early twenties

---

9. The following section on the North American context is drawn largely from Hiestand's "Pastor-Scholar to Professor-Scholar: Exploring the Theological Disconnect between the Academy and the Church," in *Westminster Theological Journal* 70 (2008): 355–69.

10. Our historical survey will focus on New England and the legacy of the "New Divinity" movement, which was ground zero for theological scholarship in the Colonial Period.

11. See Donald M. Scott, *From Office to Profession, The New England Ministry 1750–1850* (Philadelphia: University of Pennsylvania Press, 1978), 52–53.

who served as tutors in the colleges; tutorship was frequently a short-term profession, viewed as a stepping stone to the theological prestige of pastoral ministry. Even being the rector of a college could be seen as a step down from the pastorate.[12] Historian George Marsden recounts the difficulty of Yale College in its attempts to replace former rector Timothy Cutler. After two years of vacancy, the trustees of the college were still "working their way through a list of Connecticut ministers but could pry none from their parishes."[13] This dialectic between pastor and tutor created an environment in which, in the main, pastors formulated theology and the tutors transmitted this theology to the students.

Further, it was the pastoral community rather than the colleges that provided the most important means of theological education for prospective clergy. Young men seeking clerical occupation would frequently attend college (a two-year program in those days) and then pursue "finishing school" under a practicing pastor in one of the "schools of the prophets."[14] Inasmuch as the pastoral and theological communities were not distinct, these schools provided training in theological studies as well as the practical aspects of ministry. A young clerical candidate would seek out an apprenticeship with a respected clergyman, and the arrangement would usually result in the student living with the pastor and his family. The theological training was heavily weighted toward systematic theology, included the study of Greek, church history (mostly Reformation and post-Reformation study), and provided the opportunity for pastoral candidates to spend hours "reading divinity" with their mentors.[15]

Participation in one of the "schools of the prophets" was often more important for clerical placement than a college education. If forced to choose between the two, many young men would opt for the former. Indeed, such post-college training was a virtual requirement for young men pursing pastoral ministry in New England. Historian David Kling notes that "in nearly every case [of Yale College graduates] those young men attracted to the New Divinity sought further training at the home of a

12. George Marsden, *Jonathan Edwards: A Life* (New Haven: Yale University Press, 2003), 110.

13. Marsden, *Edwards*, 101.

14. Marsden, *Edwards*, 32. For more on these schools, see also D. G. Hart and R. Albert Mohler, "Introduction," in *Theological Education in the Evangelical Tradition*, ed. Hart and Mohler (Grand Rapids: Baker, 1996), 15; as well as David W. Kling, "New Divinity Schools of the Prophets," in *Theological Education in the Evangelical Tradition*, 129–47.

15. Marsden, *Edwards*, 32. See also Hart and Mohler, *Theological Education in the Evangelical Tradition*, 15.

New Divinity cleric."[16] In short, the pastoral community in New England contained the theological gravitas of the day.

In many respects, the eighteenth-century dominance of the clerical theologian in New England parallels the larger narrative of the church in the fourth and fifth centuries. The institutionalization of the churches in North America outstripped the pace at which the colleges and universities institutionalized. Insofar as institutionalization and vocation tend to go together, the church was able to provide more vocational support for theologians than the academy. But this did not last.

The close of the eighteenth century saw at least three factors that significantly contributed to an undermining of the pastor-theologian paradigm. The first was the urbanization and secularization of American culture. Towns became cities, and cities became too big for a single church. The monopoly that once guaranteed clerical power over civil affairs was broken. Laws requiring church attendance — once standard in Congregational New England — became unenforceable. As American culture became more diverse and cosmopolitan, the clergy — who had long occupied a place of prominence in both the secular and religious spheres of colonial life — began to lose their political and cultural significance;[17] with it went their theological influence.

Second, an egalitarian impulse swept the nation after the American Revolution, calling into question learned professions of all kinds — but especially those of clergy, law, and medicine.[18] Nathan Hatch, in his important work, *The Democratization of American Christianity*, shows how the basic impulses that drove the Revolution tended to undercut class distinctions and the former social hierarchies of American culture. In the same way that the colonists revolted against the political establishments of England, insisting upon the equality of the citizen and the king, so too American society revolted against the religious establishments — particularly in New England — and insisted upon the religious equality of the congregant and the pastor. Neither kings nor theologians were

---

16. David W. Kling, *A Field of Divine Wonders: The New Divinity and Village Revivals in Northwestern Connecticut, 1792–1822* (University Park, Penn.: Pennsylvania State University Press, 1993), 29.

17. Scott, *Office to Profession*, 28–29, 58–59, 72–75. Scott records the cultural and political shifts, both within evangelicalism and outside of it, that gave rise to the demise and restructuring of clerical influence in wider North American culture.

18. See Nathan Hatch, *The Democratization of American Christianity* (New Haven: Yale University Press, 1989), 27–30. Hatch observes insightfully that both law and medicine have been able to regain much of their former social status; clergy have not.

needed any longer; people who could govern themselves could read the Bible for themselves. Hatch observes, "This stringent populist challenge to the religious establishment included violent anticlericalism, a flaunting of conventional religious deportment, a disdain for the wrangling of theologians, an assault on tradition, and an assertion that common people were more sensitive than elites to the ways of the divine."[19]

This anticlericalism was especially acute during the Second Great Awakening and in its aftermath. A myriad of Christian sects and denominations exploded during this time. Populist (and popular) preachers such as Lorenzo Dow, Francis Asbury, Alexander Campbell, and Joseph Smith founded new churches while decrying the dead learning of the established clergy; they insisted on a return to a more pristine, apostolic age of direct access to the divine, unencumbered by the distracting speculations of the theologians. Their egalitarian message was received enthusiastically by a large swath of the American populace, and the massive success of the Second Great Awakening within the wider American culture did much to undercut the native connection between theological learning and pastoral ministry. In North America, a theological education was no longer a necessity — indeed, was often a liability — to a successful ministry career.

And finally, the evangelical divinity schools were founded in the midst of this cultural shift. Beginning with Andover in 1808, and followed by Princeton in 1812, theological training previously accomplished via the schools of the prophets was gradually replaced by institutional training in the divinity schools. The combination of the new divinity schools, coupled with the antitheological impulse of wider evangelicalism, contracted theology into the academic context, where it still retained a vital, albeit chastened, role. By the mid-nineteenth century, the pastor theologian in North America had been replaced by the professor theologian.

Mitigating Factors in a Theologian's Vocation

A full account of why Christian theologians have, throughout history, chosen to inhabit one vocation over another is beyond the reach this book. The cultural, political, and even economic factors at work here are complex. Yet the following matters of consideration seem to span both contexts and are particularly worthy of note.

---

19. Hatch, *Democratization*, 22.

Institutional Support: Patronage and Community

James Davison Hunter, in his landmark book *To Change the World*, discusses at length the way in which cultural change comes about. Central to his thesis is the idea that cultural change has historically happened wherever "we find a rich source of patronage that provided resources for intellectuals and educators who, in the context of dense networks, imagine, theorize, and propagate an alternative culture."[20] To substantiate this claim, Hunter offers a sweeping account of history—beginning with the early church on through the Enlightenment—showing how in each case cultural change came about through networks of intellectual elites working to form new institutions. These new institutions then provided the resources and patronage to further the agenda of the initial change agents.[21] In our estimation, Hunter is almost certainly correct. While Hunter's primary thesis relates to political and cultural change, his key insight about the importance of institutions and networks has relevance for the vocational shift of the theologian from the church to the university.

Theologians do not generally produce a product that is immediately saleable to the larger public. As such, theologians need benefactors—institutional or personal—who believe in the value of their labor and who are willing to compensate them for their efforts. The "Greek" schools of the earliest theologians provided such support—even if modestly. The institutionalization of the church under Constantine provided even more support, as evidenced by the large number of theologians that moved into the churches during the fourth and fifth centuries. Likewise, the communal living of the medieval monasteries offered theologians a viable means of sharing the expense of texts that would not have been possible for isolated clerics. And as is clear in our present context, the academy offers (to use Hunter's language) the "richest source of patronage" and institutional support for theologians, especially when considered against the alternative of the local church.

Beyond the need for raw material patronage, Hunter's analysis of cultural change underscores the importance of relationships and networks.[22] Here again one finds a parallel to our current discussion. The theological enterprise is—at root—a conversation. As such, a community of conversation partners is vital to the theological task. The monasteries, cathedrals,

---

20. James Davison Hunter, *To Change the World: The Irony, Tragedy, and Possibility of Christianity in the Late Modern World* (Oxford: Oxford University Press, 2010), 77–78.

21. For Hunter's historical analysis, see chapter 5 of *To Change the World*, 48–78.

22. See Hunter, *To Change the World*, 42–43.

and universities were not simply important as financial patrons, but also as a means of networking a community of theologians without which theological conversations could not happen. Again, in our present context, such networks exist almost exclusively in the academy.

In sum, it is the institutional structure of the university that provides the primary patronage to theologians, as well as helps to facilitate a community of intellectual peers. As such, it should not surprise us that contemporary theologians have moved into the universities. If the church is unwilling or unable to provide such support, theologians will continue to look to other vocational contexts for help with the theological task.

Cultural and Intellectual Prestige

Beyond a quest for institutional support, theologians have also been drawn to the institutions with the highest degree of cultural and intellectual prestige. In the first and second centuries, the schools patterned after the classical Greek model were attractive homes for Christian intellectuals insofar as such schools represented the cultural center of intellectual life in the Greco-Roman world. As such, it was natural that Christian intellectuals like Justin adopted this vocational platform. But as the church institutionalized—especially during and after the reign of Constantine in the fourth century—the bishop's office became a center of cultural and political power unseen in previous generations. This rise in prestige coincided with a rise in clerical theologians. Likewise, the medieval monasteries and the early universities were institutions attended with intellectual and cultural gravitas. And while the university and the monasteries drew many theologians away from the church, these later institutions did not immediately result in a mass exodus from the church; all three institutions—university, monastery, and church—retained a respectable level of cultural prestige until the Enlightenment. But once the church lost intellectual prestige in the wider culture, theologians no longer moved toward the church or the monasteries as the obvious vocational context for theological scholarship. It was the secular university that ultimately became the center of intellectual prestige, and thus, it was to the schools that theologians migrated.

The narrative in North America runs in similar fashion. North American theologians remained in the pastorate for as long as the pastorate represented the high point of intellectual and cultural power. But as the pastoral vocation diminished in cultural prestige—especially during the beginning and middle of the nineteenth century—North American theologians ceased to view the church as an obvious vocational context. Increasingly, they moved toward the academy, which in nearly every way had come to replace the church as the contemporary center of intellectual influence.

The movement of Christian theologians toward centers of cultural and institutional prestige should not surprise us, nor should we view this movement as a nefarious "will to power." We should be grateful that Christian theologians occupy centers of cultural power, and it makes sense that we position ourselves in places where the gospel has the most leverage to affect wide change in people's lives. Yet one wonders if perhaps theologians have been too driven by a quest for cultural prestige. It is, of course, impossible to assign motive on a mass scale, and no doubt most Christian theologians today reside in the academy simply by default; the academy is the institution that provides the most resources and support for the theological task. But certainly at least some theologians in the academy would reject the pastoral vocation based, at least in part, on the fact that it does not occupy the same intellectual prestige as that of a university or divinity school professor. Framed in a somewhat pejorative manner, Christian theologians know that the path to intellectual prestige does not pass through the pastorate.

Conclusion

Whatever the reason, times have changed. By any account, a who's who list of the most important theologians of the past half century shows the contemporary predominance of nonclerical theologians: Karl Barth, John Webster, George Lindbeck, Wolfhart Pannenburg, John Milbank, Robert Jenson, Colin Gunton, Jürgen Moltmann, Elizabeth Johnson, Stanley Hauerwas, Hans Küng, etc. The list goes on, and the absence of clergy is notable. Today, we find ourselves in a context where to be a theologian is, almost by definition, to be a professor in the academy. And to be a pastor is, almost by definition, to be anything *but* a theologian. The exceptions to this general trend are two recent scholar popes—Benedict XVI and John Paul II. And, of course, Barth spent time as a pastor early in his career. But overall, the general trend is consistent, especially within evangelicalism; theologians no longer—in the main—reside vocationally in the churches.

But does it really matter? As long as we have Christian theologians doing good Christian scholarship (and we do), then what difference does the vocational context make? Should we care that Christian theologians have moved from the churches to the schools? Indeed, we should. To postmodernity, social location, and the next chapter we turn.

CHAPTER 4

The Theological Anemia
of the Church

It is always a suspicious phenomenon when leading churchmen ... are heard to affirm, cheerfully and no doubt also a bit disdainfully, that theology is after all not their business.[1]   *Karl Barth*

New York Times columnist Ross Douthat is one of the more articulate voices of late to draw our attention to a troubling feature of American culture. On the one hand, America "remains the most religious country in the developed world, as God-besotted today as ever; a place where Jesus Christ is an obsession, God's favor a birthright, and spiritual knowledge an all-consuming goal." Yet on the other hand, "it's also a place where traditional Christian teachings have been warped into justifications for solipsism and anti-intellectualism, jingoism and utopianism, selfishness and greed."[2] Despite our Christian heritage and religious devotion, America is awash in what Douthat calls "bad religion," patterns of belief and behavior that are defective not only theologically but ethically.

Sadly, what Douthat says of America could equally be said of evangelicalism. All is not well. Consider a few sobering facts. Divorce rates among evangelicals are not substantially better than the culture at large; the sexual ethics of evangelical singles are virtually indistinguishable from their non-Christian counterparts; and avarice and greed are now so common that we gaze at our excesses without blinking.

Of course, there has never been a golden age of Christian piety; every generation has its blights. But as James K. A. Smith puts it, when the only difference between Christians and non-Christians is that Christians go to church while non-Christians stay home and read the paper, you know something is amiss.[3]

---

1. Karl Barth, *Evangelical Theology: An Introduction* (Grand Rapids: Eerdmans, 1979), 40.

2. Ross Douthat, *Bad Religion: How We Became a Nation of Heretics* (New York: Free Press, 2012), 4.

3. James K. A. Smith, *Desiring the Kingdom: Worship, Worldview, and Cultural Formation* (Grand Rapids: Baker, 2009), 208.

What has contributed to the moral laxity of evangelicalism? Surely, the answer is complex, not cookie-cutter. Yet who will deny that *a failure of belief* is at least partly to blame? For what we believe about God, ourselves, and the world inevitably informs our vision of the good life. And this vision in turn shapes our desires, which then direct our actions. It is because a man truly believes his bride will make him happy that he desires her and thus wills to marry her. And it is because a man truly believes a mistress will make him happy that he desires her and thus wills to leave his wife.

Augustine articulated this centuries ago in terms of the *ordo voluntatis*, the order of the will. First belief, then love, then action. Love, Augustine argued, drives action by setting the will into motion. Yet love does not arise in a vacuum; it emerges out of our belief about the Good. For Augustine, we ultimately desire that which we believe is in our own best interest. Yet this belief can be right or wrong. When our belief concerning the Good is in keeping with the truth—namely that union with God is in our own best interest—our affections and our wills are rightly ordered. But when our belief is misplaced, our affections and our wills are likewise misplaced.

For Augustine, God has given human beings a mind so that they can "become capable of knowledge and of receiving instruction, fit to understand what is true and to love what is good."[4] He continues, "It is by this capacity [i.e., the capacity to understand] the soul drinks in wisdom, and becomes endowed with those virtues by which, in prudence, fortitude, temperance, and righteousness, it makes war upon error and other inborn vices, and conquers them by fixing its desires upon no other object than the supreme and unchangeable Good."[5] For Augustine then, a key to right living is to grow in one's capacity to rightly believe and understand the true nature of the Good.[6]

---

4. Augustine, *City of God*, 22.24.

5. Augustine, *City of God*, 22.24. Ultimately Augustine is most concerned about the movement of the will with respect to God, but his way of framing the relationship between belief, desire, and ethics extends throughout his way of describing the entire human experience.

6. This is not the place to offer a full account or defense of the Augustinian position. Yet a few comments in anticipation of a critique along the lines of James K. A. Smith in his *Desiring the Kingdom* are in order. In his book, Smith critiques the idea that human beings should be conceived of primarily as "believing" creatures. Such a picture, Smith argues, tends to frame human beings in rationalistic terms that inadvertently deemphasize the import of the body. Smith argues instead that the defining thing about human beings is not what we think, or even what we believe, but what we *love*, what we *desire*. Smith goes on to insist that more than mere beliefs shape our desires; desires are "shaped, primed and aimed by liturgical practices that take hold of our gut and aim our heart to certain ends" (40). We are in agreement with Smith's primary concern, namely that human beings are shaped by more than the mere transmission

It is here that the discipline of theology plays such a vital role in Christian formation. Much of the hard work of theology is to examine, self-consciously and critically, both the conscious and subconscious beliefs that shape and govern human activity. Theology attempts to make sense of the world in which we live, of God, and of ourselves. It teases out the connections between ideas and actions and helps to create new ways of imagining reality — ways that are distinctly Christian, or, we might say, distinctly *real*. At root, Christian theology attempts to say right things about God, ourselves, and our world in ways that shape true belief and orient human beings toward their proper purpose.

This orienting task of theology is vital insofar as many things compete to shape human belief. Our past experiences, our relationships, our bodies, our habits — all of these send us messages about who we are, who God is, and what it means to live the good life. And as is the case in this fallen world, these messages are often mixed. Our bodies tell us to believe one thing about the good life. Our relationships another. Our experiences a third. Our ingrained habits yet a fourth.[7] It is precisely here, at the intersection of these competing messages, that the theologian must step in and sort things out.

The theologian seeks to grasp and then articulate the central message of the gospel in such a way that the gospel becomes the norm by which all the various messages are judged worthy or unworthy of belief. The theologian seeks to unravel and shed light on the intricate web of beliefs — both conscious and unconscious — that shape our vision of the world and, thus, our desires and ultimately our actions. A chief task of the theologian is to peer beneath the surface and identify the mistaken beliefs that give rise to misplaced affections and subsequent erring ethics. Ideas have consequences, and it is the theologian's job to sort out these consequences.

The theologian occupies a crucial — even foundational — leadership role within the church. This does not mean that the theologian is solely responsible for healing all the ethical ills of the church. As noted above,

---

of information, and that the body is a vital component in influencing what we love. But we do wish to emphasize, perhaps more so than Smith (and in keeping more faithfully, we believe, with the New Testament connection between faith [i.e., "belief"] and obedience) the foundational role that beliefs play in shaping desires and, thus, ultimately the will. As such, theology — the primary task of which is to help shape belief — will perhaps retain more of a central role in our view of discipleship than it may for some who follow Smith's emphasis on liturgy.

7. Articulating such a robust account of the will is a chief burden of James K. A. Smith in his two books on liturgy and Christian formation. See his *Desiring the Kingdom* and his *Imagining the Kingdom: How Worship Works* (Grand Rapids: Baker 2013).

there are many factors that shape beliefs. It will take more than the discipline of theology itself to bring about life change. Ultimately, the church—through its Word, sacraments, liturgy, people, and most of all its Head—contains the full panoply of resources necessary for shaping belief in a properly Godward direction.

Yet the theologian uniquely bears the responsibility to identify and direct the resources of the church—to sort out how, and in what ways, these various belief-shaping resources of the church must be brought to bear on the people of God. The theologian acts as a sort of spiritual director, helping the church navigate belief with a view to love and good deeds. Notably, when theologians falter at their task, the people of God are handicapped in finding their way to right belief. And when beliefs go astray, desires are misplaced, and ethics stumble.

Faltering Theology, Faltering Ethics: Who's to Blame?

Insofar as ethics are ultimately connected to beliefs, and insofar as it is the job of theology to shape beliefs, the ethical anemia of evangelicalism is due in no small part to an underlying theological anemia. It's not simply that we have failed to apply the properly proscribed cure; worse, we are not even sure of the diagnosis. We have embraced wrong beliefs regarding anthropology, epistemology, cosmology, soteriology, etc. A reductionist and companionate view of marriage has fueled divorce rates; a recreational view of sex mixed with Cartesian mind-body dualism has led to a cultural breakdown of the Christian definition of marriage; a postmodern rejection of metanarratives has undermined belief in the uniqueness and sufficiency of the Christian gospel; a Gnostic antimaterialism has infiltrated Christian cosmology in a way that encourages either greed or asceticism. These are all mistaken beliefs about distinctly *theological* matters. To put not too fine a point on it, evangelicals are floundering ethically because we are floundering theologically.[8]

Given the faltering of evangelical theology, one might be tempted here to cast a suspicious glance at evangelical academic theologians. After all,

---

8. Here, we agree with David Wells's critique of contemporary evangelicalism. In a book-length argument, Wells draws a causal connection between the collapse of evangelical theology and the collapse of evangelical ethics. See his *No Place for Truth; or, Whatever Happened to Evangelical Theology?* (Grand Rapids: Eerdmans, 1993). So too Christian Smith traces the connection between belief and actions in his book *Soul Searching: The Religious and Spiritual Lives of American Teenagers* (Oxford: Oxford University Press, 2009).

isn't it the job of academic theologians to ensure the theological integrity of the church? But the theological—and corresponding ethical—floundering of contemporary evangelicalism cannot be laid at the feet of our academic theologians.

Evangelical theology has increasingly flourished since the middle of the twentieth century. As evangelicalism emerged out of the modernist-fundamentalist controversies, evangelical scholars and theologians developed a deepening and robust theology. Leading lights like J. Gresham Machen, Benjamin Warfield, Harold Ockenga, Carl F. H. Henry, George Eldon Ladd, J. I. Packer, and others did much to construct a coherent and meaningful theology that was at once faithful to the faith, intellectually robust, and appropriate to its time. And contemporary evangelical theologians and scholars such as Mark Noll, Kevin Vanhoozer, Kevin Hector, N. T. Wright, D. A. Carson, and Alister McGrath have provided evangelicals a robust theological integrity and coherence in the face of postmodernity. While perhaps not addressing every need in the most user-friendly manner, evangelical theologians have done a remarkable job servicing the overall theological needs of the church. Evangelical theology, as a discipline, has much to be thankful for.

How can it be, then, that while evangelical theologians in the academy have matured and deepened (and they have, in our estimation, genuinely matured and deepened), the church has increasingly lost its way theologically? The answer is surprisingly simple. Pastors, not professors, are the theological leaders of the church.

Despite assumptions to the contrary, the pastoral office retains the burden of the church's theological leadership, regardless of the vocational context of professional theologians and scholars. Or to say it again, the burden of maintaining the theological and ethical integrity of the people of God is inevitably linked to an *office within the church,* not to a *group of people with intellectual gifting.* Insofar as pastors bear the day-to-day burden of teaching and leading God's people, they simply *are* the theological leaders of the church. As goes the pastoral community, so goes the church.[9] Assuming sufficient tenure, show us a pastor with robust theological depth, and we'll show you a local church with a corresponding theological depth. Likewise, show us a pastor who lacks the capacity to think meaningfully

---

9. Thomas Oden speaks rightly when he says that clergy "represent the unity, continuity, and integrity of the community of faith." Oden, *The Rebirth of Orthodoxy: Signs of New Life in Christianity* (New York: HarperCollins, 2002), 121.

about the gospel, and we'll show you a church that lacks the same. It doesn't matter how theologically informed the pastor's professor is. The theological integrity of a local church will not rise above that of its pastor. What is true for individual churches is true for the church as a whole.

The theological anemia of the church, and its corresponding ethical anemia, rests squarely on the shoulders of a theologically anemic pastoral community. Not every pastor need be a theologian, of course; many are gifted in other vital ways. But collectively, the pastoral community is responsible for deftly shepherding the people of God to embrace the core truths of the gospel. And it is here that the pastoral community—in the main—is failing. The pastoral community is no longer endowed with the sort of theological capacity it once had—a capacity that is necessary for shaping the beliefs of the church in healthy ways.

David Wells sounded the alarm on this point nearly twenty years ago. Lamenting the atheological state of the North American clergy, Wells observed, "I have watched with growing disbelief as the evangelical Church has cheerfully plunged into astounding theological illiteracy. Many taking the plunge seem to imagine that they are simply following a path to success, but the effects of this great change in the evangelical soul are evident in every incoming class in the seminaries, in most publications, in the great majority of churches, and in most of their pastors."[10] Taken as a whole, we pastors have lost our way theologically, and those we shepherd have followed us into the ditch. Sadly, the theological anemia of the pastoral community has not prevented us from making theological judgments; it has only prevented us from making *coherent* theological judgments.

Rejecting the intrinsic connection between theology and praxis, the evangelical pastoral community that emerged out of post-Revolutionary America has been, in many instances, bereft of both. Philip Schaff, decrying the theological vapidity of American pastors during his day, wrote, "Every theological vagabond and peddler may drive here [in America] his bungling trade without passport or license, and sell his false ware at pleasure. What is to come of such confusion is not now to be seen."[11] The

10. Wells, *No Place for Truth*, 4. See also David Wells, *God in the Wasteland: The Reality of Truth in a World of Fading Dreams* (Grand Rapids: Eerdmans, 1994), and David Wells, "Educating for a Counter Cultural Spirituality," in *Theological Education in the Evangelical Tradition*, ed. D. G. Hart and R. Albert Mohler (Grand Rapids: Baker, 1996), 290–99.

11. Philip Schaff, *The Principle of Protestantism as Related to the Present State of the Church*, trans. John Nevin, (Chambersburg: Publication Office of the German Reformed Church, 1845), 116.

demise of pastoral theological integrity, and the corresponding collapse of Christian ethics in the twenty-first century, is the full flowering of the bud that Schaff saw in his day. Pastors have ceased to traffic in ideas, yet ideas still have consequences.

Many, of course, are the voices—both within and outside the church—calling for pastors to once again take seriously their responsibility as the theological leaders of their local congregations. Such calls, however, have gone largely unheeded by the pastoral community. The reason, we believe, is that evangelicals have contented themselves to work within the present division of labor that exists between the academy and the church. In the present division, pastors are viewed primarily as theological middlemen between academic theologians and congregants. This vision of pastoral ministry, however well intentioned, ultimately masks the inherently theological nature of the pastoral vocation and perpetuates the chronic theological anemia within the church.

Pastors as Theological Middle Management: A Mistaken Division of Labor

Wells, perhaps as much as anyone in recent years, has argued vigorously that evangelicalism must recover its theological integrity if it hopes to survive in the modern world. In a single sustained argument spanning several books, Wells charts the slow demise of evangelical integrity in North America and calls for the church once again to embrace theology as a primary cure for our ethical ills.[12] Evangelical theology has, Wells argues, become too preoccupied with guild concerns.

Yet Wells does not lay the blame solely on the shoulders of the learned guilds in the academy. Theology, Wells argues, properly takes place at the intersection of several worlds. "First, there is the world of learning into which theology taps; second, there is the Church for who theology is constructed; and third, there are the intermediaries who, in the modern context, often become small worlds unto themselves but who must work within this matrix—scholars who mediate the world of learning and the pastors who broker what results to the churches."[13] According to Wells, a

---

12. See Wells, *No Place for Truth, Losing Our Virtue: Why the Church Must Recover its Moral Vision* (Grand Rapids: Eerdmans, 1998), *Above All Earthly Pow'rs: Christ in a Postmodern World* (Grand Rapids: Eerdmans, 2005), and *The Courage to Be Protestant: Truth-lovers, Marketers, and Emergents in the Postmodern World* (Grand Rapids: Eerdmans, 2008).

13. Wells, *No Place for Truth*, 6.

breakdown has occurred insofar as pastors no longer embrace their role as "brokers" of theological truth. Evangelicals have "redefined the pastoral task such that theology has become an embarrassing encumbrance or a matter of which [pastors] have little knowledge."[14]

Without this vital link between the academy and the church, theology in the academy has become cut off from its rightful audience; theologians are no longer able (or compelled) to construct theology for the life of the church. Evangelical theology has lost its way and become preoccupied with academic guild concerns; and the churches, led by a pastoral community that no longer conceives of itself in theological terms, has lost its distinctive Christian ethical framework. The results, Wells notes, "are unhappy."

In most every way, we agree with Wells's assessment. But not quite. Wells's vision of pastors as "brokers" of theological truth is commendable and certainly represents a theological promotion for pastors over contemporary notions of pastoral ministry. As noted above, the people of God in the churches depend upon their pastors to lead them well. Regardless of the rich content of evangelical theology, it is lost on the laity if it is not mediated through the pastoral community. But the vision of pastors as brokers of theological truth, while legitimate as far is it goes, does not go far enough. In our collective past, pastors did more than just "broker the results" of academic theologians to the church; they *were* the theologians.

In every new generation, the church needs a new generation of theologians and scholars. The pendulum of human fallibility moves us—sometimes slowly, sometimes quickly—between the extremes of human wisdom. And with each swing of the cultural pendulum, there is a need for a fresh examination and articulation of the church's fixed message.[15] How shall the good news of the risen Christ—his incarnation, teaching, death, resurrection, ascension, and pending return—be proclaimed in each generation? What do the great theologians of the past—Irenaeus, Athanasius, Augustine, Thomas, Calvin, Luther—have to say about the needs of the present? With what tonal inflections shall we speak into the diversity of our age? What aspect of the apostolic message most needs to be heard in our particular cultural moment? What resources does Christianity have to offer the church and wider world in light of contemporary pagan eth-

---

14. Ibid.

15. Along similar lines, Thomas Oden writes, "Cultures and languages change constantly. The same ancient memory of revelation must be attested in ever-new cultures and languages. It is a necessary feature of tradition-transmission that it both guards the original testimony and communicates that testimony effectively within dawning cultures." Oden, *Rebirth of Orthodoxy,* 42.

ics, anthropology, epistemology, eschatology, and the like? Such are the questions facing the church with every new age, and formulating cogent answers to them is the task of the church's theologians. But where do we find such theologians? Whether intended or not, Wells's paradigm would have us look primarily away from the pastorate, toward the academy. Wells is not unique here.

In the contemporary division of labor between academy and church, the underlying assumption has been that academic theologians are best positioned to provide theological leadership to the church, and that pastors are best positioned to apply this theology in a local context. Per this paradigm, when pastors need theological training or help, they are to look to the resources of the academy. Thus to be a theological pastor (indeed to be a pastor theologian) is to be a pastor who has accessed and mastered the theology produced in the academy and is capable of translating and passing it down to average folks in the pews. This basic vision is common within evangelicalism among those who see an inherent connection between theology and pastoral ministry.[16] But this vision of pastors as brokers isn't working.

The identity of pastors as brokers does not involve pastors actually constructing theology themselves. This is actually a demotion (theologically speaking) from how pastors once functioned in the church. The sweeping and near universal assumption that pastors are—at best—brokers of theological truth, while intending to raise the theological integrity of the

16. See for example, R. Albert Mohler, *He Is Not Silent: Preaching in a Postmodern World* (Chicago: Moody, 2008), 105–14. See also the twin essays by John Piper and D. A. Carson in *The Pastor as Scholar and the Scholar as Pastor: Reflections on Life and Ministry*, eds. Owen Strachan and David Mathis (Wheaton, Ill.: Crossway, 2011). It is clear throughout both essays that Piper and Carson view the identity of the pastor almost exclusively within the framework of the broker-theologian model. So too Kevin Vanhoozer, who uses the analogy of pastors as local directors, helping ensure that the doctrinal script written by the church's theologians is performed in the local church. See his *The Drama of Doctrine: A Canonical-Linguistic Approach to Christian Theology* (Louisville: Westminster John Knox, 2005), 448–55. Likewise, David Read, in his essay, "What Pastors Can Teach Theologians," works within the standard division of labor, arguing that pastors must help theologians be ecclesial, while theologians must help pastors be theological. See David H. C. Read, "What Pastors Can Teach Theologians," in *The Pastor as Theologian*, eds. Earl E. Shelp and Ronald H. Sunderland (New York: Pilgrim Press, 1988), 88–105. In a like vein, the stated aim of a prominent mainline pastor-theologian program (now decommissioned) was to seek "for ways to let the best theological research and thought of our time [conceived of in almost exclusively academic terms] find its way into the 'the bloodstream of the Church.'" Brian Daley, quoting Wallace Alston, director of the Center for Theological Inquiry's Pastor-Theologian Program in "Saint Gregory of Nazianzus as Pastor and Theologian" in *Loving God with Our Minds: The Pastor as Theologian*, eds Michael Welker and Cynthia A. Jarvis (Grand Rapids: Eerdmans, 2004), 119.

pastoral community, in many ways only serves to perpetuate the myth that theology is an essentially academic enterprise. The broker vision pushes pastors into a fundamentally second-tier, middle-management role with respect to theology. Per this vision, pastors are no longer expected to generate fresh theological syntheses in light of contemporary intellectual challenges; this is the role of theologians in the academy. We pastors are to appropriate and disseminate the results of theological scholarship, not actually engage in it ourselves.

In a review of Tom Wright's *Justification: God's Plan, Paul's Vision* (which is a response to Pastor John Piper's book on the same topic), church historian Gerald Bray chastises Wright for producing a book that has "let us down badly" and is "full of digressions, personal anecdotes which appear to have no purpose other than to win sympathy for the author, and random attacks against unnamed people who are supposed to be typical of popular modern Evangelicals." In short, Bray didn't care for the book. Wright, of course, can deal with his own critics. But it's worth noting Bray's concluding comments. He writes,

> If anything is clear from Bishop Wright's book, it is that it is impossible to serve two masters at the same time. Either one is a diocesan bishop or one is a serious scholar—having a day job in Auckland Castle and pottering around with scholarship in one's spare time is not a viable option in today's world. Bishop Wright pleads lack of time for what even he recognizes is the inadequacy of his response to Mr. Piper, but if that is so, he needs to reconsider his priorities. There is no shame in giving up scholarship, or in resigning a bishopric, when the pressures become too great, but doing a half-baked job in one is bound to lead to the suspicion that one is doing an equally half-baked job in the other, and that the long-suffering recipients of such treatment are ending up with the worst of both worlds.... Let us hope and pray that he will see this for himself and decide whether he wants to be a bishop or a scholar—but not both.[17]

Ouch. The sentiment Bray espouses above is typical of those both within and outside the academy. Theological scholarship is not the domain of the pastorate; leave that to the professionals in the academy. Having

---

17. Gerald Bray, "The Righteousness of God," in *The Churchman*, vol. 123.2 (2009): 104. Bray's comments here are, of course, as equally disparaging to Pastor Piper as they are to Bishop Wright. Given that Bray doesn't also admonish Pastor Piper to "stop pottering around with scholarship," one suspects that Bray's comments have less to do with Wright's vocation and more with the fact that he disagrees with Wright's position.

thus been reduced to second-tier status, pastors no longer view theological education as a vital aspect of their training. Sustained theological engagement after seminary—even middle-management-level engagement—is not always easy to find within the pastoral community. None of this is surprising, given the fact that we have told pastors to content themselves with occupying the passive role with respect to theological scholarship.

But despite the bifurcation between pastoral ministry and theology, the pastoral vocation remains vested with the theological leadership of the church. The pastoral community may conceive of itself as middle management, but this does not change the fact that pastors are the theological chief executive officers of the church. What God has joined together is not so easily separated.

Again, our grievance here is not with Wells's broker vision, as such. Brokering theological truth to a local congregation is the job of every pastor. What's more, we do not believe that most pastors are called to do more than this. But it has been manifestly unwise of the pastoral community—collectively—to embrace a *mere* middle-management position with respect to the church's theological leadership. The burden and responsibility of supplying the church with robust theological syntheses lies with the pastoral community, not the academy. At least some pastors must pass beyond the broker vision and move to the supply side of the theological enterprise.

Academic theologians have much to offer the church, but it is to our folly and the church's harm that we pastors have tried to outsource the entire theological enterprise to the academy. The result has been like a man driving a bus who is under the mistaken impression that he has delegated the responsibility of driving to his friend seated next to him. Compounding matters, his friend, rather than insisting that he actually take up the responsibility native to his position, perpetuates the wrong impression. This is a great way to end up in the ditch. And "end up in the ditch" we have.

No doubt the North American pastoral community still suffers from a post-Revolutionary hangover. But the general egalitarian impulse in North America of the late eighteenth and early nineteenth centuries was not exclusively an assault on the *pastor* theologian; it was an assault on professional theologians wherever they might be found—both academic and pastoral. And it is notable that while evangelical theology has made a comeback in the academy, it has not recovered in the church. Again, the social and cultural factors at work here are complex. But certainly, a primary reason that the pastoral community has not experienced the same theological recovery is precisely because we evangelicals have embraced the mistaken belief that theology is largely an academic discipline. It is telling that the statement "he is a theologian" is now most naturally understood to mean "he is a professor." If we intend to reference a theologian who is a pastor, we say, "He is a pastor theologian." It is the professor, not the pastor, who has become the default theologian of evangelicalism.

Conclusion

As long as both church and academy fail to realize that the burden of theological leadership inevitably lies with the church's pastors, pastors will tend to neglect this primary duty of their calling and the church will suffer from a chronic theological anemia. Again, not every pastor must be a theologian. But new measures must be taken to reawaken the collective consciousness of the pastoral community regarding its inherent and unavoidable role as the theological leader of the church. Designating the pastoral community as brokers is not sufficient. But before moving forward to the "new measures," we must first address one additional challenge regarding the demise of the pastor theologian.

Not only has the demise of the pastor theologian adversely affected the theological integrity of the church, it has likewise affected the ecclesial integrity of theology. Theological scholarship, no longer taking place primarily within the institution it was intended to serve, has lost its way and become ecclesially anemic.

CHAPTER 5

The Ecclesial Anemia of Theology

Did the university location change my theology? I think it did, because
here the demand to be "scholarly" or "scientific" made by the other
faculties was greater than it had been in a college belonging to the
church.[1]   *Jürgen Moltmann*

Gerald recalls that when he was a graduate student, he discussed possible
employment with an associate pastor of a large metropolitan church, who
during the course of their conversation lowered his voice, leaned in closely,
and said, "The fact is, they're not real big on the seminary around here.
You can sometimes get the impression they'd rather hire guys straight out
of the marketplace. We've just seen too many young guys coming out of
the academy, able to parse Greek verbs, and discuss process theology, but
having no real idea what the church is about."

As Gerald continued in the interview process, the supervisor of the
department in which he would be working prepared him for his interview
with the executive staff. "You should be ready to explain why you got an
MA in theology," he said, in a rather serious and matter-of-fact way. "That
might raise some red flags."

His comments, though unsettling, were not surprising. Since the
inception of the evangelical seminary in North America—beginning
with Andover in 1808 and followed by Princeton in 1812—pastors and
laity have long lamented the disconnect between "academic" scholarship
and the theological needs of ecclesial ministry.[2] Simply put, the theology
coming out of the academy is often not viewed by pastors and parishioners
as particularly relevant or necessary for ecclesial life and ministry.[3] Though

---

1. Jürgen Moltmann, *Experiences in Theology: Ways and Forms of Christian Theology*, trans.
Margaret Kohl (Minneapolis: Fortress, 2000), 7–8.

2. See Donald M. Scott, *From Office to Profession: The New England Ministry 1750–1850*
(Philadelphia: University of Pennsylvania Press, 1978), 124–25, as well as Gary Scott Smith,
"Presbyterian and Methodist Education," in *Theological Education in the Evangelical Tradition*,
eds. D. G. Hart and R. Albert Mohler (Grand Rapids: Baker, 1996), 88–93. Both works recount
the frustration that has historically existed between the academy and the local church.

3. See R. Albert Mohler, "Thinking of the Future, Evangelical Education in a New Age,"
in *Theological Education in the Evangelical Tradition*, 278–79, as well as Richard J. Mouw,

often overstated, this unfavorable assessment of academic theology has been difficult to shake.

The critique of academic theology comes from within the academy as well. Oxford theologian Alister McGrath, in a work on the future of evangelical theology, recounts his personal experience with the occasional irrelevance of academic theology. He writes,

> I recall an occasion back in the 1970s when a leading British theologian gave an address to a group of us who were preparing for ministry in the Church of England.... He related how he regularly had to visit little old ladies in his parish, and was obliged to converse with them over cups of lukewarm over-brewed tea. We all politely tittered (as we were clearly meant to) at the thought of such an immensely distinguished theologian having to suffer the indignity of talking with little old ladies whose subject of conversation was grandchildren, the price of groceries and the pains of old age. After his lecture, we wished he had spent rather more time with these people. The bulk of his lecture was unintelligible, and made no connections with real life—the issues of relationships, the cost of living, and the pain of the world. It was academic in the worst possible sense of the word.[4]

McGrath goes on to note that evangelical theology in North America, despite its pragmatic bent, has not escaped the accusation that it is too far removed from the "real needs" of the local church. Too often, "much recent theology seems to focus on issues which appear to be an utter irrelevance to the life, worship and mission of the church."[5] In many ecclesial settings, theological sophistication has become synonymous with theological irrelevancy. Those of us who share a concern for theological reflection understand the significant, indeed necessary, role theology plays in the life of the church. And the careful work of evangelicalism's academic theologians has been a blessing to the church. But the migration of Christian theologians away from the pastorate into the academy has been, we believe, at the root of the frustrations surrounding the relationship between the academy and

---

"Challenge of Evangelical Theological Education," in *Theological Education in the Evangelical Tradition*, 285. Both men discuss the increasing dissatisfaction among evangelical laity for sustained theological education in a formal academic setting.

4. Alister E. McGrath, "Theology and the Futures of Evangelicalism," in *The Futures of Evangelicalism: Issues and Prospects*, ed. Craig Bartholomew, Robin A. Perry, Andrew West, and Alister E. McGrath (Leicester: Inter-Varsity Press, 2003), 17–18.

5. McGrath, "Futures of Evangelicalism," 19.

the church. The historically new academic social location of contemporary theologians presents at least two challenges.

First, the questions being addressed in the academy, legitimate as they may be, are not always the same questions being asked by pastors on the ground. Pastors and professors do not occupy the same vocational social location; for this reason, these two groups are faced with different vocational pressures and needs. The migration of theologians to the academy and away from the pastorate has resulted in a dearth of theologians available to answer distinctly ecclesial questions from distinctly ecclesial vantage points.

And second, evangelical theology, insofar as it is now almost an entirely academic enterprise, is often constrained by guild-specific rules that frequently discourage theological engagement on explicitly Christian matters. At their founding, the universities were informed by a Christian framework that shaped the methodological framework of the schools and made ample room for doxological and ecclesiological projects. But in the wake of modernity, the larger university context is no longer—in the main—a hospitable home for evangelical Christian belief (or even orthodox belief generally). This has tended to push much of evangelical theology into an apologetically constrained and pastorally muted posture. This is especially true in the fields of church history and biblical studies but can also be seen in theology proper. We explore these two challenges in turn.

The Academy and the Church: Diverging Social Locations

It is now almost universally recognized that social location profoundly influences theological reflection. Because theology is an attempt to appropriate the truth of Scripture in light of life's questions, each theologian's theological paradigm cannot help but be heavily influenced and directed by the particular questions that arise from his or her unique social location. It was the backdrop of Old Calvinism's unwillingness to preach the gospel indiscriminately that led to Jonathan Edwards's important distinction between moral and natural ability, paving the way for the gospel preaching that so typified the Great Awakening. And it was Luther's immersion in the functionally semi-Pelagian soteriological paradigm of medieval scholasticism that caused him to rethink the doctrine of justification by faith. In these instances, the unique social location of each theologian raised important concerns that subsequently directed their labor of theological reflection. As Daniel Migliore appropriately notes, "The concrete situation of theology helps to shape the questions that are raised and the priorities that are set."[6]

Postmodernity, for all of its shortcomings, has reminded us that our seemingly neutral ways of looking at a given data set are not as neutral as we might think. Unable to fully disentangle ourselves from our own particular contexts, we view the world through a unique set of epistemic lenses; God alone has the bird's-eye view. These lenses not only influence what we see but also our "first thoughts"—the presuppositions and questions we bring to the epistemic task.[7] We no longer assume the ability to perch neutrally above our theological investigations; we are deeply embedded within and shaped by our own social location.

Philosopher Hans-Georg Gadamer goes further. Gadamer argues not only that neutrality is impossible, it is actually a barrier to the epistemic process. Taking issue with the modern assumption that entanglement in one's respective social location can only have a negative epistemic effect, Gadamer argues (rightly, in our mind) that it is in fact our *very personal relation* with the object that actually provides our way to understand the object. For Gadamer, "Prejudices are not necessarily unjustified and erroneous, so that they inevitably distort the truth. In fact, the historicity of our existence entails that prejudices, in the literal sense of the word, constitute the initial directedness of our whole ability to experience. Prejudices are biases of our openness to the world. They are simply conditions whereby we experience something—whereby what we encounter says something to us."[8] In fact, attempts to gain some personal remove from the subject at hand—what Gadamer calls "controlled alienation"—work against our ability to know as we ought. "What kind of understanding does one achieve through 'controlled alienation'? Is it not likely to be an alienated understanding?"[9]

We need not exaggerate the significance of social location. Perhaps Gadamer does at certain points; undoubtedly, postmodernity has at many points. Yet even conservative critics who reject postfoundational epistemologies readily acknowledge "that all interpretations of Scripture are shaped

6. Daniel L. Migliore, *Faith Seeking Understanding: An Introduction to Christian Theology* (Grand Rapids: Eerdmans, 1991), 14.

7. Kevin Vanhoozer, *First Theology: God, Scripture and Hermeneutics* (Downers Grove, Ill.: InterVarsity, and Leicester: Apollos, 2002), 19. For Vanhoozer, "first thoughts" (or prolegomena) involve the questions that each theologian brings to the theological task.

8. Hans-Georg Gadamer, *Philosophical Hermeneutics*, trans. David E. Linge (Berkley: University of California Press, 2008), 9.

9. Gadamer, *Philosophical Hermeneutics*, 27.

by the context of the interpreter."[10] Postmodernity, though not the first epistemologically focused age to recognize the importance of social location, has appropriately brought to the fore an element of theological formation that was present yet underemphasized in the modernist theological systems of old. The advent of feminist theology, black theology, liberation theology, and queer theology (to name a few) is the natural outworking of the contemporary emphasis on social location. And it is our postmodern context that helps us see that what we now generally call "theology" is actually a certain kind of theology, namely *academic* theology—a unique kind of theology developed and sustained within an academic social location and driven by academic questions and concerns.

As theologians moved from pulpits to classrooms, their theological aims and aspirations couldn't help but shift as well. For the demands of university life are different than the pressures of pastoral ministry, even as delivering a lecture is different than preaching a sermon, discussing a text different than administering the sacraments, or writing a scholarly article different than counseling the downtrodden or visiting the sick. This is not to say that one is easy, the other hard. Nor is it meant to suggest there is no overlap between the two social locations and their attendant practices. And, of course, many academic theologians invest heavily in their churches.

But with that said, we should not make the opposite mistake of downplaying the influence of one's vocational setting and pressures, whether as a scholar or pastor, whether in the academy or church. To put it bluntly, what you do to earn a paycheck and put food on the table is formative, perhaps in ways you don't fully appreciate. Here one is reminded of Jesus' insight, "Where your treasure is, there your heart will be also" (Luke 12:34).

The fact is that academic theologians have to deal with institutional pressures and vocational priorities that may have little direct relevance to the church. This is true even for those serving at Christian colleges. We were visiting over lunch with a well-known evangelical New Testament

---

10. D. A. Carson, "Domesticating the Gospel: A Review of Grenz's *Renewing the Center*," in *Reclaiming the Center: Confronting Evangelical Accommodation in Postmodern Times*, eds. Millard J. Erickson, et al. (Wheaton, Ill.: Crossway, 2004), 32. For more on recent conversations within evangelicalism regarding social location and epistemology, see Stanly J. Grenz, "Articulating the Christian Belief-Mosaic: Theological Method after the Demise of Foundationalism," in *Evangelical Futures: A Conversation on Theological Method*, ed. John G. Stackhouse Jr. (Grand Rapids: Baker, and Leicester: Inter-Varsity, 2000), 107–19; David K. Clark, *To Know and Love God: Method for Theology* (Wheaton, Ill.: Crossway, 2003), 153–56; Vanhoozer's "The Voice and the Actor: A Dramatic Proposal about the Ministry and Minstrelsy of Theology," in *Evangelical Futures*, 75–86; and J. P. Moreland and Garret De Weese, "The Premature Report of Foundationalism's Demise," in *Reclaiming the Center*.

scholar who worked at a Christian school and who had written a number of popular-level works. His books had been well received, but his peers in the academy cautioned him against too much "of that sort of thing." Writing too many popular-level books about explicitly pastoral concerns ran the risk of damaging his reputation as a genuine scholar.

While no two institutions are the same, it is certainly the case that a vocation as an academic, even in a divinity school, is different than a vocation as a pastor. This was pressed home to us when we finished schooling and entered ministry. Intellectually and theologically, there was a great deal of overlap between our theological education and our roles as pastors, but the fit was not exact.

The foci of theology in the academy often did not address the very real and pressing theological needs of our congregations. How many scholarly and theological works have you seen on premarital sexual boundaries? Or on parenting? Or on doubt, idolatry, discipleship, or marriage? There are some, but not many. These sorts of topics tend to be addressed on an exclusively popular level and do not generally capture the attention of those in the academy. Yet these sorts of topics are massively important for the people of God, and it is a disservice to the church to treat such topics only in popularizing sort of ways.

The fact that academic theology does not always map directly onto the needs of the church is not a critique of academic theology. The academic context is a legitimate social location, with its own legitimate questions. But we must more consciously acknowledge that the academy and the church represent two different worlds, with different sets of questions. It has been a mistake to place all of our intellectuals into the academic social location, while leaving the specifically ecclesial questions unaddressed or underaddressed.

The Academy and the Church: Diverging Theological Methods

The problem goes further. Beyond the different questions of each context, the *way* theologians and scholars are taught to do theology in the academy often runs counter to the needs of pastoral ministry. The secular university runs on methodological agnosticism, but this stymies pastoral insights before they can reach the light of day; if you play by the rules, you are unable to voice genuinely ecclesial concerns.

The tensions created by the respective social locations of the academy and the church are further exasperated by the generally hostile posture of the university to Christian belief. Though the early universities—both in Europe and North America—were distinctly Christian, modern universities are not. This relatively recent development (post-Enlightenment in Europe, and the early twentieth century in North America) has created new vocational pressures for academic theologians—even for those theologians working within distinctly confessional institutions and divinity schools.

On the whole, the marginalization of Christian belief within the academy has tended to push evangelical theology into a defensive, and at times, pastorally muted, posture with respect to its liberal and secular counterparts. Migliore gets to the heart of our concern when he writes, "Each social location of theology imposes its own set of questions ... its own special emphasis. Theology in the academic context naturally tends to be apologetically oriented."[11] Apologetically oriented theology is appropriate and necessary. But it is not sufficient for meeting all the theological needs of the Christian community. A brief look at the North American narrative illustrates the point.

Early North American theologians were nearly all pastors, and the majority of early theological reflection in North America was directed toward distinctly ecclesial matters.[12] Historian George Marsden notes that even as late as 1840, four out of five denominational college presidents were ordained clergy, as were two-thirds of university presidents. The professorship as a distinct profession had only begun to emerge, and the ecclesial community still retained a significant amount of theological influence over the colleges and universities.[13]

Yet the breaking of the European Enlightenment on American shores eroded the Christian foundations of the divinity schools and the larger American university system. The evangelical understanding of Scripture was forcibly confronted by the deconstructive assault of the higher critics and an overweening confidence in modern science. North American seminaries began to abandon orthodoxy; theological education became

---

11. Migliore, *Faith Seeking Understanding,* 14.

12. For a full recounting of the North American narrative, see George Marsden, *The Soul of the American University: From Protestant Establishment to Established Nonbelief* (Oxford: Oxford University Press, 1994), which details the transition from a distinctly Christian North American university context to a now established context of nonbelief. See also his insightful shorter work, *The Outrageous Idea of Christian Scholarship* (Oxford: Oxford University Press), 1997.

13. Marsden, *Soul of the American University,* 81. Marsden goes on to observe that the vast majority of colleges were evangelical until 1870.

increasingly secular. To remain respectable in the eyes of a secularizing academic community as well as a secularizing culture, the survival of the evangelical faith became closely linked to the defense of Scripture. As seminaries divided down hermeneutical lines, those schools that remained orthodox were compelled to develop a specific theology in light of their liberal counterparts. North American theological reflection was no longer a strictly internecine conversation.

The fault lines dividing the divinity schools stretched into the larger North American university context. The universities, which had begun as distinctly Christian institutions, gradually lost their Christian identity and eventually reinvented themselves as bastions of secularism.[14] The distinctly evangelical ethos of the schools was largely gone by the 1920s, and the liberal Protestantism that replaced it was itself moved to the margins by the late twentieth century. Marsden notes the result:

> Teachers of religion in seminaries and in many church-related colleges ... have been confronted with a dominant university culture in which explicit religious perspectives, or at least explicit Christian perspectives, are increasingly considered unscientific and unprofessional.... Even though many academics are religious, they would consider it outrageous to speak of the relationship of their faith to their scholarship. That is true not only in religious studies, but also in almost every discipline, no matter how relevant religious beliefs might potentially be to academic interpretation.[15]

Marsden is here writing at the close of the twentieth century. More than fifteen years later, things remain much the same, except that postmodernism, for all its hang-ups, has rightly scuttled much of the modern project that gave birth to the established nonbelief of the North American universities. In many respects, this has opened new avenues of dialog for previously marginalized groups; yet openness to a distinctly "Christian" voice remains marginal in most university contexts.[16]

---

14. Compulsory chapel services could still be found at state-run schools until 1950, and even up until 1960, almost all American universities were explicitly Christian, even if mainline liberal. See Marsden, *Soul of the American University*, 3.

15. Marsden, *Outrageous Idea*, 6–7.

16. Marsden observes that Christian scholars, particularly those of an evangelical or conservative variety, have not benefited from the newfound openness to previously marginalized voices. See Marsden, *Soul of the American University*, 430. No doubt this is because Christians have long occupied the power position within North American universities; as such, we are viewed as the voice that must be suppressed to make room for the previously oppressed. But Marsden rightly notes that this has resulted in an overcompensation, where now nearly any perspective is legitimate except a distinctly Nicene Christian perspective.

As a consequence, North American evangelical academic theologians still often find themselves in an established, sometimes hostile, wider academic community that can at times seem "to have more to do with elitism, ideological warfare and rampant antireligious propaganda than with the advancement of learning or excellence."[17] An open, evangelical, pastoral agenda is often not looked upon with favor by the secular academy.

Insofar as evangelical theologians have entered into the wider academic discussions, apologetically oriented theology has become normative to evangelical thought in a way not seen in the early days of North American evangelicalism.[18] It would be unfair to suggest evangelical academic theology is *merely* or *only* (or even *primarily*) apologetic in nature. Yet certainly a great deal of intellectual energy that used to be spent developing evangelical theology is now being redirected toward defending evangelical theology.[19]

Further, inasmuch as evangelical academic theologians vie for a place at the wider academic table, they are in some measure forced to play by preestablished rules — rules that often implicitly or explicitly require them to suppress their Christian commitments. We live in community. And not only does each unique community shape our theological reflection, it serves as the primary sounding board for our theological scholarship. Each audience has its own set of rules, presuppositions, relational dynamics, dominant personalities, and cultural taboos. Audience drives, and sets the bounds for, theological reflection. Given the posture of the wider academic environment, evangelical theologians often find themselves formulating theology within the constraints set by the liberal and secular academy, constraints that are often at odds with a distinctly Christian project.[20] These constraints are felt across the various theological guilds.

---

17. McGrath, *Futures of Evangelicalism*, 25–26.

18. Compare for example, contemporary theologies such as David K. Clark's, *To Know and Love God: Method for Theology,* and John Fienberg's *No One Like Him: The Doctrine of God* (Wheaton, Ill.: Crossway, 2001), with early evangelical treatises such as Jonathan Edwards's *Freedom of the Will* or his *The End for Which God Created the World.* The difference in social location is readily discerned. Compare also recent commentaries such as William Lane's *Hebrews,* 2 vols., Word Biblical Commentary 47A-47B (Dallas: Word, 1991), with John Brown's commentary on the same epistle. The latter's more pastoral and in-house evangelical focus becomes quickly apparent.

19. In this vein, A. B. Caneday laments the lengths to which evangelical theologians have gone in responding to the epistemic agnosticism of postmodernity, suggesting that evangelical theologians are "occupying themselves more with *methods* for doing theology than with *doing* theology." A. B. Caneday, "Is Theological Truth Functional or Propositional: Postconservatism's use of Language Games and Speech-Act Theory," in *Reclaiming the Center*, 137.

20. Caneday notes that the desire among evangelical theologians to maintain "theological correctness" in the face of the wider academic community "tends to intimidate and shape Christian theological action, speech and thought" (Ibid., 138).

New Testament scholarship must now address form and source criticism, but expertise in such fields, though necessary for defending evangelical orthodoxy, is, as D. A. Carson notes, "of only minimal help to the interpreter."[21] The battles of higher criticism are hard fought and, when won, allow us to merely hold the ground upon which we were already standing. Evangelical historians feel the press of this as well. Those who discuss the Great Awakening, for example, must do so within the pre-established antisupernatural framework that governs such a topic. The very concept of a wide-scale spiritual awakening is questioned and, when acknowledged at all, is frequently attributed to social, political, or economic factors.[22] Working within such constraints, though perhaps necessary when dialoging with the wider academic community (and perhaps not always even then), makes it difficult for the evangelical historian to draw explicitly evangelical applications from historical events such as the Great Awakening, the Reformation, etc.[23]

Similar constraints fetter the intellectual historian's task as well. The postmodern refusal to pass judgment on the moral worth of the other, combined with the modern ideal of the disinterested observer, has significantly hampered our ability to speak prophetically in the realm of historical doctrine. Within the wider academic world, any attempts at moral evaluation are viewed as "improper" to the historical task.[24] The

---

21. D. A. Carson, et al., eds., *An Introduction to the New Testament* (Grand Rapids: Zondervan, 1992), 45.

22. For example, historian Susan Juster looks to sexuality as an explanation for the Great Awakening. She writes, "The key to Whitfield's phenomenal success as a revivalist lay in his ability to fuse female passions with the language of consummation" (Susan Juster, "The Spirit and the Flesh: Gender, Language, and Sexuality in American Protestantism," in *New Directions in American Religious History*, eds. Harry S. Stout and D. G. Hart [Oxford: Oxford University Press, 1997], 342).

23. Martyn Lloyd-Jones, discussing the study of historical revivals such as the Great Awakening, writes, "We are not interested in [revivals] merely from the historical standpoint.... There is no point in reading about revivals just for the sake of reading the history in the stories. No, our motive and our interest must be to read and to study and to consider what has happened in the past, in order that we may discover the great principals that underlie this matter, in order, in other words, that we may discover what it is that we should be seeking and praying for in our own day and generation. It should be a utilitarian, rather than an antiquarian interest and motive that should govern us." Martyn Lloyd Jones, *Revival* (Wheaton, Ill.: Crossway, 1994), 93. Such a perspective is certainly out of step with wider academic historical studies and even has a certain dissonance within evangelical academic circles.

24. McGrath follows this precedent in his magisterial work on the doctrine of justification, *Iustitia Dei: A History of the Christian Doctrine of Redemption*, 2nd ed. (Cambridge: Cambridge University Press, 1998). In his discussion regarding Lutheranism's later modification of Luther's theology, McGrath writes, "It would be improper to inquire as to whether this ... modification was justified; it is however right and proper to note that it took place" (219). See also page 395 for his concluding comments, which reflect a similar sentiment.

articulation of bare history, not moral evaluation with a view to contemporary concerns, serves as the only legitimate historical method.[25] Such an approach makes the appropriation of a Luther, Aquinas, or an Augustine quite difficult. Rather than studying Augustine to know what the *church* should believe, Augustine must now be studied to know what *Augustine* believed. Though there are certainly difficulties inherent in any attempt to appropriate the thought of a past thinker for contemporary application, who better than our intellectual historians to understand the ramifications of classic doctrinal debates and their significance for contemporary ecclesial discussions? Yet the wider academic concern for methodological agnosticism often prevents such gains.

The challenge of the modern university context is not a distinctly North American Protestant concern. Joseph Ratzinger (himself a former academic theologian, then cardinal, then pope), in his *The Nature and Mission of Theology,* draws upon the work of Italian historian G. Alberigo and observes insightfully about the European context, "The fact that the university became the new seat of research and of the teaching of theology without a doubt enervated its ecclesial dynamism and furthermore severed theology from vital contact with spiritual experiences."[26] Ratzinger's observation that contemporary theology is often "enervated of its ecclesial

---

25. See James E. Bradley and Richard A. Muller, *Church History: An Introduction to Research, Reference Works, and Methods* (Grand Rapids: Eerdmans, 1995), 11–25 for a discussion regarding the progression of historical method. Mueller and Bradley, themselves Christian historians, argue for a form of methodological agnosticism for the Christian historian.

26. Joseph Ratzinger, *The Nature and Mission of Theology: Essays to Orient Theology in Today's Debate* (San Francisco: Ignatius, 1995), 115–16. Ratzinger is drawing from Alberigo's "Sviluppo e caratteri della teologia come scienza," in *Cristianesimo nella storia II* (1990), 257–74. Ratzinger's concerns are hardly isolated. For similar sentiments germane to biblical studies, see Craig Bartholomew's, "Table in the Wilderness? Towards a Post-Liberal Agenda for Old Testament Study," in *Making the Old Testament Live: From Curriculum to Classroom,* eds., R. Hess and G. Wenham (Grand Rapids: Eerdmans, 1998), 19–47, and Michael C. Legaspi, *The Death of Scripture and the Rise of Biblical Studies* (Oxford: Oxford University Press, 2012), 155–69. Voicing sentiments similar to Bartholomew and Legaspi, Kevin Vanhoozer laments the bare historicism that plagues much of the academic biblical-studies guild, noting that there is a "near consensus among biblical scholars that there is no place for doctrine in the exegetical inn.... One is hard pressed to say which is uglier: the ditch separating theory and practice or the ditch that separates exegesis and theology." *The Drama of Doctrine: A Canonical-Linguistic Approach to Christian Theology* (Louisville: Westminster John Knox, 2005), 20. Alister E. McGrath makes similar observations regarding the discipline of theology in his, "Theology and the Futures of Evangelicalism," in *The Futures of Evangelicalism,* 17–29. For a look at the historic church/academy disconnect in North America, see Scott, *From Office to Profession,* 124–25; Smith, "Presbyterian and Methodist Education," 88–93; and Gerald Hiestand, "Pastor-Scholar to Professor-Scholar: Exploring the Theological Disconnect between the Academy and the Local Church," in *Westminster Theological Journal,* vol. 70 (2008): 360–66.

dynamism" is undeniably true, even if not universally so. While this need not be overstated, it is the lamentable reality that Christian theologians now often find themselves pressured, for guild-specific reasons, to limit the pastoral impulses that might otherwise drive their work. The inevitable result is a theological project that often fails to terminate in doxology and true Christian formation. As Ratzinger goes on to observe, "A theology wholly bent on being academic and scientific according to the standards of the modern university, cuts itself off from its great historical matrices and renders itself sterile for the Church."[27]

The situation is perhaps not as dire when one considers the professors of evangelical colleges and divinity schools; many such professors operate self-consciously as theologians and scholars in service of the church, and their theological context provides the freedom to reflect this commitment. Yet the methodological agnosticism of the wider university is not without effect, even in the divinity schools. Wells rightly observes that the contemporary standard of scholarship is set by the wider universities. While confessional schools grant more freedom than the universities, "It is in the [university] guild that the canons of learned credibility are established. And insofar as these canons divert reflection from the traditional function of theology, they contribute to its continued breakdown."[28] It does not take one long to note the difference between the earnest, pastoral tone of a Calvin or Luther and the more "disinterested" tone one often finds in a contemporary academic journal of theology—even explicitly evangelical journals.

Insofar as evangelical scholars are called to the wider academic conversation, it is appropriate that he or she respect (and respectfully challenge) the rules that govern the dialog. Yet evangelical theology misses out when the best and brightest of our scholars consistently subject the best and brightest of their reflections to secular rules of engagement. Theological formation is a project that "belongs first and foremost to the people of God ... the proper and primary audience for theology is therefore the Church, not the learned guild. Whatever this guild might contribute to the life and construction of theology is to be gratefully received, but the university fraternity is not its primary auditor."[29]

---

27. Ratzinger, *The Nature and Mission of Theology*, 116.
28. David Wells, *No Place for Truth; or, Whatever Happened to Evangelical Theology?* (Grand Rapids: Eerdmans, 1993), 127.
29. Ibid., 5.

An apologetically focused theology, though essential, forms only the outer ring of the theological enterprise. It defends the structure, but it is not itself the whole structure. Certainly, we must continue to advance a robust evangelical presence in the wider academic community; evangelical academic theology must continue. But we must also recognize that being forced to play within the present academic boundaries limits the ecclesial impact of academic theology.

Conclusion

Academic theologians have much to offer the church. But it has been a mistake for pastors to adopt a primarily passive role with respect to the church's theological leadership. The pastoral questions of the church need pastoral answers, and it is the burden of pastors to provide them. However much we might prefer the standard division of labor that views pastors as "brokers," at least some pastors must once again embrace the inevitable burden of theological leadership associated with their vocation. The native home of theology is the church, and the responsibility of the church's theological leadership lies with the pastoral community.

This does not mean that every pastor must engage in theological scholarship or feel burdened to produce fresh theological syntheses for the wider church. But it does mean that the pastoral community—taken as a whole—must once again embrace the burden of theological leadership that rests squarely on our shoulders.

Yet the contemporary currents run in the opposite direction. Many graduate and postgraduate students feel pulled mutually toward a career as a theologian and a career in the church. Finding the road forked, they are constrained to choose between the two. Generally, such individuals move into the academy, thinking that it is easier to be a pastorally active theologian than it is to be a theologically active pastor.

And who can blame such logic? The church has ceased to provide a vocational context for clergy to function as productive theologians. As such, we have, for the past one hundred and fifty years, siphoned the best and the brightest minds away from the pastorate into the academy. The "broker of truth" vision implied in the current division of labor is not sufficient to inspire those with robust intellectual gifting to move into the pastorate. Those who aspire to robust theological leadership will not (and should not) content themselves with middle management.

At root, the problem does not lie with the academy or our academic theologians. The church has been blessed, and will continue to be blessed, by faithful academic scholars. The problem is not that we have academic theologians; the problem is that we no longer—in the main—have pastor theologians. Or to put it more precisely, we no longer have the sort of pastor theologians representative of our past—the sort capable of reimagining the pastoral vocation along theological lines.

CHAPTER 6

The Pastor Theologian: A Taxonomy

> For insofar as we are determined to be true theologians, we think
> within the community of God's people, and for that community, and in
> the name of that community; — how shall I say it? — we think as a part
> of the community itself.[1]   *Helmut Thielicke*

In the previous two chapters, we detailed the negative effects on the church
that have come about through the bifurcation of the theologian and the
pastor. In sum, this divorce has led to the theological anemia of the church
and the ecclesial anemia of theology. What, then, might be the solution to
these twin dilemmas?

Our answer, of course, is a recovery of the pastor theologian. The
return of theologians to the pastorate addresses the theological anemia
that has plagued pastoral ministry since the Enlightenment. This, in turn,
provides a vital and now-missing resource for deepening the theological
integrity of the people of God and, most importantly, anchoring mature
Christian ethics. And likewise, the return of pastors to the theological task
helps to inject an ecclesial voice into theological conversations, thus pulling
Christian theology back into its native orbit of the church.

But what *is* a pastor theologian anyway? Of course, every pastor is the
primary theologian of his congregation. And so in one sense, every pastor
is a pastor theologian. But true as this may be, such broad definitions
ultimately render the identity of the pastor theologian meaningless. (If
every day is a holiday, no day is a holiday.)

While we certainly agree that every pastor must (indeed, inevitably
does!) provide theological leadership to his local congregation, the aim of
our book is not to insist that every pastor must be a pastor theologian. As
stated previously, the pastoral office requires a variety of gifts and skills. In
the same way that all pastors are called to preach the gospel, irrespective of
whether they are uniquely gifted in evangelism, so too all pastors are called
to provide theological leadership to their local congregations, irrespective
of whether they are uniquely gifted in theology.

---

1. Helmut Thielicke, *A Little Exercise for Theologians* (Grand Rapids: Eerdmans, 1952), 4–5.

Our vision then, of the pastor theologian, is directed toward a certain subset of the pastoral community. And, indeed, this is generally in keeping with contemporary notions of the pastor theologian. In the common vernacular, the term *pastor theologian* is primarily used to refer to those within the pastoral community who have unique theological interests and gifting. For many, the term refers to a pastor whose study is filled with reference books. For others, the term refers to a pastor who writes a theological blog or publishes sermons. For others, it refers to a pastor who has a PhD or who has a certain kind of preaching ministry (namely, a theological one). And for many, it simply refers to a really smart pastor.

These current conceptions of the pastor theologian—however legitimate—are insufficient for the sort of ecclesial and theological recovery we have in mind. A fresh vision is needed. Toward this end, we propose here a return to an ancient vision of the pastor theologian—the sort of pastor theologian who not only engages with theology as an end-user, but who also constructs and disseminates theology for the broader church.

To clarify our vision of the pastor theologian, we propose in this chapter a threefold taxonomy of the pastor theologian: the pastor theologian as *local theologian*, the pastor theologian as *popular theologian*, and the pastor theologian as *ecclesial theologian*. The local theologian is a pastor theologian who constructs theology for the laity of his local congregation. The popular theologian is a pastor theologian who provides theological leadership to Christian laity beyond his own congregation. And the ecclesial theologian is a pastor theologian who constructs theology for other Christian theologians and pastors.

As will become apparent, the local theologian and popular theologian are already active in contemporary evangelicalism. The ecclesial theologian, however, is a lost paradigm. Resurrecting this model is the aim of this book and the focus of this chapter. Yet in our effort to resurrect the pastor theologian as ecclesial theologian, we simultaneously wish to affirm the vital necessity of the local- and popular-theologian paradigms; each is a legitimate and important identity of the pastor theologian.

In recounting the local theologian and popular theologian then, we wish to both affirm the vital role they play and set a context for identifying and resurrecting the ecclesial theologian. Understanding the interrelatedness of these three types of pastor theologians will enable the academy, the church, and the emerging generation of pastors and theologians to envision new possibilities for what the pastor theologian can be, as well as enable future pastors and theologians to identify themselves with the paradigm that best fits their gifts and calling.

The Pastor Theologian as Local Theologian

There is no single definition within evangelicalism for the term "pastor theologian." But perhaps the most common conception of the pastor theologian is that of a local theologian to one's own congregation. In this model, the pastor theologian is a theologically astute pastor who ably services the theological needs of a local church. This theological leadership is most immediately accomplished through a theologically rich preaching ministry but also through theologically thick pastoral care, counseling, and organizational leadership. A local theologian has a solid working knowledge of the primary Christian doctrines and is able to draw connections between biblical truth and lived experience. Such pastors are inevitably readers and lifelong learners; they are reflective and thoughtful and understand that ideas have consequences — not least theological ideas. They are frequently looked to by other pastors and those in their congregations for guidance and direction on theological matters. Theological study comes easy to them, and they engage in it as a life-giving font of personal renewal.

A robust working vision of the pastor as local theologian can be found in Kevin Vanhoozer's *The Drama of Doctrine*. In his work, Vanhoozer helpfully offers us an account of Christian doctrine that draws upon the imagery of the theatre. The gospel, Vanhoozer rightly argues, is something to be performed, not merely believed. Doctrine "is a condensed form of Christian wisdom, rooted in the Scriptures and accumulated over the centuries, about how rightly to participate in the drama of redemption."[2] Canonical doctrines are thus like "stage directions" that provide instructions for the church's performance of the gospel.[3]

Keeping with the theater metaphor, Vanhoozer likens the pastor to the "director" of a local performance of the gospel.

> The Father is the playwright and the producer of the action; the Son the climax and summation of the action. The Spirit, as the one who unites us to Christ, is the dresser who clothes us with Christ's righteousness, the prompter who helps us remember our biblical lines, and the prop

2. Kevin Vanhoozer, *The Drama of Doctrine: A Canonical-Linguistic Approach to Christian Theology* (Louisville: Westminster John Knox, 2005), 448.

3. Ibid., 18, emphasis added.

master who gives gifts (accessories) to each church member, equipping us to play our parts. While the Holy Spirit is the primary director who oversees the global production, *it is the pastor who bears the primary responsibility for overseeing local performances.*[4]

For Vanhoozer, the pastor is an "assistant director" (working under the Spirit), who ensures that a local Christian community is performing the gospel according to the stage directions of canonical doctrine. Given that doctrine provides the stage directions for the performance, it is vital that the "directing" duties of the pastor be carried out with careful attention to doctrine. Theology, "far from being an obstacle to pastoral ministry (as per the common misconception) ... is in fact its servant."[5] Vanhoozer rightly notes how Scripture, creedal theology, and confessional theology all serve as necessary signposts that help maintain continuity between a local performance and the Spirit-directed universal performance. Thus, "pastors who neglect Scripture become disoriented and lose the way of the gospel. Pastors who neglect creedal and confessional theology disinherit and dispossess themselves and their congregations of the accumulated dramaturgical wealth of the church."[6] In short, when pastors fumble their lines, congregations lose their way.

Notably, the local theologian's primary scope of responsibility is his own congregation.[7] The local theologian is neither burdened with nor called to theological leadership to the wider Christian community. Writing theological scholarship — whether popular or beyond — is not a vital component of the local theologian's identity. It is the sermon, more than anything else, that serves as the primary canvas for the local theologian's theological art. Al Mohler articulates this vision well when he writes, "The health of the church depends upon pastors who infuse their congregations with deep biblical and theological conviction, and the primary means of this transfer of conviction is the preaching of the Word of God."[8]

The vision of the pastor as local theologian is needed today, and would

---

4. Ibid., 448.

5. Ibid., 449.

6. Ibid., 454–55.

7. "Pastors owe it to their congregations, as a matter of moral obligation of their vocation, to be persons of study." Gordon Lathrop, *The Pastor: A Spirituality* (Minneapolis: Fortress, 2011), 101.

8. R. Albert Mohler, *He Is Not Silent: Preaching in a Postmodern World* (Chicago: Moody, 2008), 111.

that more pastors embraced the theological burden of leading their own congregations.[9] As we have argued in the previous chapter, the health of the church is directly tied to its theological integrity, and its theological integrity is directly tied to the theological integrity of its shepherds. The people of God are desperate for pastors who are able to deftly and thoughtfully help them understand the ways in which the gospel and its implications impact all areas of life. It is the duty of the pastor, beyond all others, to feed and shepherd those assigned to his care. However else this theological leadership might be extended, it is the sheep within one's own fold that must occupy pride of place. The local theologian understands this burden and is uniquely qualified to consciously embrace his role as the necessary and inevitable theologian of his congregation.

The Pastor Theologian as Popular Theologian

Encompassing the local theologian model, and then expanding it, we arrive at a second identity of the pastor theologian — the pastor theologian as *popular theologian*. The popular theologian is a local theologian, yet with a broader range of influence. In this model, the pastor theologian is a pastor who writes theology, an activity not inherent to the identity of the local theologian. Bridging the gap between the professional theological community and the local church, the popular theologian translates academic theology down to other pastors and the laity.[10]

---

9. Vanhoozer's articulation of the pastor theologian as a theologically astute pastor who shepherds a local congregation is in keeping with others who advocate the pastor-theologian model. See the twin essays by John Piper and D. A. Carson in *The Pastor as Scholar and the Scholar as Pastor: Reflections on Life and Ministry,* eds. Owen Strachan and David Mathis, (Wheaton, Ill.: Crossway, 2011). See also John Nevin's *The Reformed Pastor: Lectures on Pastor Theology* (Eugene, Ore.: Pickwick, 2006). So also R. Albert Mohler, *He Is Not Silent: Preaching in a Postmodern World* (Chicago: Moody, 2008), 105–14. For a similar vision of the pastor theologian in the mainline tradition, see in Wallace M. Alston and Cynthia A. Jarvis, eds., *The Power to Comprehend with All the Saints: The Formation and Practice of a Pastor-Theologian* (Grand Rapids: Eerdmans, 2009), and Michael Welker and Cynthia Jarvis, eds., *Loving God with Our Minds: The Pastor as Theologian* (Grand Rapids: Eerdmans, 2004). So also Gordon Lathrop, in his wonderful book, *The Pastor: A Spirituality* (Minneapolis: Fortress, 2011), 101–8. And in many ways, David Wells's "broker" vision maps closely on to the local theologian model (though Wells's model can include the popular theologian model as well). See Wells, *No Place for Truth* (Grand Rapids: Eerdmans, 1993), 6, 221, 245.

10. Here Wells's conception of pastors as "brokers" of theological truth has relevance. Wells does not explicitly call for "brokers" to actively engage in a writing ministry, but certainly such a ministry would be consistent with his vision of the pastor as theological translators between the "professional" and congregants.

Many pastor theologians of this variety have postgraduate degrees, read widely in theology, and serve as significant and necessary voices in contemporary Christianity. Generally, however, their theological writing is not an attempt to enter into the theological discussions taking place among professional theologians and biblical scholars. Rather, it is an effort to help other pastors and the laity better understand the importance of relevant issues in theology.

Thus, in the popular theologian model, the job of the pastor theologian is to unpack the complexities of Nicene Trinitarianism, Chalcedonian Christology, the Reformed confessions, atonement theories, and the like, in ways that are accessible to the average pastor and person in the pew. Commentaries written in this genre tend to be devotional and focused on application. Theological works tend to be introductory. Popular theologians also tend to address issues not covered by academic theologians — topics such as dating, parenting, marriage, finances, church leadership, and liturgy. In short, popular theologians speak to issues at a popular level that tend to be left under- or unaddressed by academic theologians, as well as translate academic theology down into the common vernacular of the local church. As with linguistics, the translation work done by popular theologians requires a specialized skill in its own right. Thinking in both worlds, popular theologians are able to bring profound truth to bear on the lives of average people in ways that affect true and lasting change.

Like the local theologian, popular theologians are vital to the health of the church. Theology that cannot be translated and applied to the laity is of little use to the church (and arguably is not good theology at all!). It is the popular theologian who embraces this role of translator, for the good of God's people.

But both of the above pastor theologian models, however important — and they are important — do not exhaust the full range of possibilities for the pastor theologian. Central to our concern is that neither does full justice to the vital role that pastors inevitably play in leading the church theologically. Limiting the pastor theologian paradigm to the local and popular theologian models runs into the same problem as Wells's "broker" vision. For as long as the term *pastor theologian* is limited to local and popular theology, the emerging generation of theologians — who have an inherent desire to engage in theological scholarship at the highest levels — will not view the pastorate as the best way to fulfill their sense of theological calling. The local and popular theologian models, as valuable as they are, have not served as sufficiently compelling visions for pulling theologians back into the churches. This inevitably pushes many of our brightest divinity students away from the pastorate and toward the academy, thus perpetuating the chronic disconnect noted in the previous chapter. Evangelicalism will never reclaim the emerging generation of theologians for the pastorate if our only conception of the pastor theologian is that of a local or popular theologian.

Pastors such as Irenaeus, Athanasius, Augustine, Calvin, and Edwards were more than local or popular theologians (though they were often those as well). Their theological systems represented the critical thought of their day. It is this kind of pastor theologian that must once again become a viable option for a future generation of clergy.

Enter the pastor as ecclesial theologian.

The Pastor Theologian as Ecclesial Theologian

If the church is plagued by theological anemia, and theology is plagued by ecclesial anemia, then we need the sort of pastor theologian capable of redressing both ills. The ecclesial theologian is such a pastor theologian.

An ecclesial theologian is a *theologian* who bears shepherding responsibility for a congregation and who is thus situated in the native social location that theology is chiefly called to serve; and the ecclesial theologian is a *pastor* who writes theological scholarship in conversation with other theologians, with an eye to the needs of ecclesial community. In this way, the ecclesial theologian includes, but extends beyond, the local theologian and popular theologian models.

The pastoral duties of the ecclesial theologian will be in nearly every respect like that of the local and popular theologian. Which is to say, the pastor as ecclesial theologian is first and foremost a local church pastor who views the pastoral vocation from a theological vantage point. His theological commitments shape his sermons, leadership, pastoral care, administration, and outreach, all with a view to deepening the faith of God's people. What is more, the shepherding responsibility to ensure the theological, ethical, and missional integrity of his local congregation is the primary responsibility that frames his sense of vocation. In this sense, the pastor as ecclesial theologian is first a pastor, and only then a theologian. Or to say it again, the theological contributions of the ecclesial theologian spring from the overflow of the shepherding responsibilities that he carries for his local congregation.

Yet the ecclesial theologian is more than a theologically astute congregational leader. The ecclesial theologian is a theologian in the fullest sense of the term—one who provides theological leadership to God's *ecclesia*. With respect to his theological work, the ecclesial theologian writes theology to other theologians and scholars, drawing upon the wealth of resources found in the most enduring works of the church and in conversation with the most relevant contemporary dialog partners—both within and outside of the church. The ecclesial theologian counters the often unspoken sentiment that says, "Deep, penetrating commentaries and books on the atonement—that stuff is for the academy; pastors should stick to writing Christian living stuff for the laity." *Me genoito!* Expounding God's Word and reflecting on the nature of the atonement is the duty of bishops and elders and pastors. The ecclesial theologian represents a return to the days when pastors wrote theology that was richly theological, deeply biblical, historically informed, culturally aware, explicitly pastoral, and prophetic.

John Calvin and his *Institutes* come to mind here. Calvin's work is a fair bit different than the average modern theology text. But it is not different because it is "lighter" or "easier to read" or "pitched to a less informed audience." It is different in that it is framed according to Calvin's pastoral context, does not feel such a need to plumb the nearly endless depths of secondary literature (there wasn't as much), is not afraid to be explicitly theological and confessional, interacts with the great thinkers of the past who have helped shape orthodox thought, and—most significantly— because it prophetically calls the church to take action. We cannot dismiss the academic training that informed and undergirded Calvin's theological insights. But neither can we dismiss the way his pastoral duties at Geneva shaped his overall theology. Calvin did not change the world because he was a successful academician (though he was involved in academic discussions). He changed the world because he wrote as a robust, theologically informed, intelligent, prophetic pastor who understood—as a matter of vocation—what it was to have the weight of souls upon his shoulders. The ecclesial theologian, then, is a pastor who writes theological scholarship that is self-consciously "churchy" and explicitly Christian, and whose agenda is driven by the questions that emerge from the grind and angst of the parish context.

The question before us is complicated by the fact that the theological guild in which we envision the ecclesial theologian working has long since vanished, or perhaps better stated, has transformed itself from an ecclesial guild into an academic guild. Theology has become so thoroughly an academic enterprise that when we cast the ecclesial theologian as a pastor theologian who writes to other theologians, we are very often misunderstood to mean that the ecclesial theologian writes primarily to academic theologians. This is not what we mean. We are not here proposing that the ecclesial theologian simply write academic theology. A poor use of social location, that. We envision another realm of theological discourse— another dialect of theology—that is as intellectually robust as academic theology but focused on questions that are explicitly ecclesial.

In many respects, it's easy to see a distinction between the ecclesial theologian and local theologian; a theological writing ministry readily distinguishes the two. And insofar as we have framed the ecclesial theologian as a pastor theologian who writes theology to other theologians and scholars, this sets the ecclesial theologian apart from the popular theologian. But an obvious question emerges: beyond vocation, in what way does our definition of the ecclesial theologian differ from that of an academic theologian? Is the ecclesial theologian simply a pastor who writes academic theology? And if not, what sort of theological project would an ecclesial theologian pursue different than what is currently being pursued by an ecclesially sensitive academic theologian?

More clarity is needed, which is the task of our next chapter.

CHAPTER 7

The Pastor Theologian
as Ecclesial Theologian

> While the love of truth seeks the "sanctified leisure" (*otium sanctum*)
> of contemplation, the necessity of love (*necessitas caritatis*) demands
> the willing acceptance of our social and ecclesiastical obligations.
>
> *N. Joseph Torchia*[1]

In this chapter, we want to flesh out the nature of the ecclesial theologian, with special attention to the sort of theological scholarship such a person might pursue. Toward this end, we highlight eight characteristics of the ecclesial theologian's scholarship and identity, set primarily in relation to the academic theologian, with a view to resurrecting the ancient vision of the pastor as a theologian of and for the church.

1. The Ecclesial Theologian Inhabits the Ecclesial Social Location

Above all, the ecclesial theologian is a theologian who constructs theology as a vocational pastor. This is not an incidental characteristic. It is the pastoral vocation that sensitizes and positions the ecclesial theologian to make unique pastoral contributions to theology. Inevitably, the grind and press of the pastoral vocation forces one to grapple in profound ways with one's theological conclusions. A theologian's theodicy is deepened (and confronted) when he has to conduct the funeral of a six-week-old baby who was accidentally killed by his own mother when she shifted in her sleep. And one's theology of marriage is pressed and shaped in profound ways when one has to provide counsel to a husband whose wife is on her third affair, or to a woman whose husband has left (for the fourth time)

---

1. N. Joseph Torchia, "Contemplation and Action," in *Augustine through the Ages: An Encyclopedia*, ed. Allan D. Fitzgerald (Grand Rapids: Eerdmans, 1999), 233; cited in Anthony C. Thornhill, "Scholarship and Ministry in the Life and Thought of Augustine," *Eleutheria* 1:2 (2011): 107–14 (p. 111).

because of a drug addiction. And one's anthropology and views on gender are pushed beyond the facile when one has to help a man wrestle through the question of gender identity or decide whether to baptize Jane Doe who ten years ago was John Doe.

One cannot help but be shaped in profound ways by the steady rhythm of such experiences, and consequently, one's theology is likewise shaped. Pastors are not, of course, the only Christians called upon to give counsel and care in the face of such circumstances. But without question, the vocational *Sitz im Leben* of the pastorate uniquely tests and shapes one's theology in ways the vocational context of other social locations does not. As Kevin Vanhoozer rightly observes, "The church is less the cradle of Christian theology than its crucible: the place where the community's understanding of faith is lived, tested, and reformed."[2]

Here, we return to Hans-Georg Gadamer's key insight. Gadamer dispenses with modern notions of objectivity, as well as the corresponding postmodern epistemic despair associated with this loss, and instead argues (rightly, in our mind) that one's immersion in a given social location is *the very means* by which one is able to speak intelligently about that social location in the first place. Subjective placement within a context (in this case, the church) is not a liability but is indeed *the way in* for properly understanding that context.[3] The pastor is uniquely positioned to understand, assess—and address—the pressing theological/ministerial needs of the ecclesial community precisely because he stands uniquely, as a matter of vocation, *within* that community.

And not only does the social location of the pastoral vocation offer unique insight into the issues being discussed by contemporary theologians, it also unearths hitherto under- and unaddressed questions. Questions regarding family, friendship, marriage, singleness, parenting, dating, personal finance, idolatry, addiction, and more, while given some attention by academic theologians and scholars, are not given attention in due proportion to their pastoral import in the life of God's people. The ultimate *telos* of Christian theology is the edification of the church—and not simply the church in its broad universal sense (however true this might

---

2. Kevin Vanhoozer, *The Drama of Doctrine: A Canonical-Linguistic Approach to Christian Theology* (Louisville: Westminster John Knox, 2005), 25.

3. See Hans-Georg Gadamer, *Truth and Method* (New York: Continuum, 2004). The whole book, of course, lays out Gadamer's approach, but see in particular 267–98. See also his *Philosophical Hermeneutics*, trans. David E. Linge (Berkeley: University of California Press, 2008), see all, but especially 8–9.

be), but the church as comprised of individuals: the old widower, the young business executive, the married mother of children. Theology exists as a means of supporting the hard work of faith in the lives of such as these. The pastoral social location foregrounds this vital aspect of theology, and the ecclesial theologian self-consciously—and vocationally—embraces it and allows it to direct his work.

2. The Ecclesial Theologian Foregrounds Ecclesial Questions

Not only does the ecclesial theologian allow the ecclesial social location to drive the focus of his work, he likewise allows the ecclesial social location to shape his theological method. Toward this end, the ecclesial theologian, writing as a pastor, foregrounds and makes explicit the ecclesial questions that drive his project. This stands in contrast to much evangelical academic scholarship. Academic theologians are frequently driven by pastoral considerations, but in academic scholarship, such considerations are often left unexpressed (this is perhaps seen most often in biblical and historical studies). Instead, academic scholarship tends to be framed primarily as an exploration of a theoretical or historical idea. What is the right way to read Justin Martyr's posture toward paganism? Is Dunn correct that Paul saw the Jewish Law chiefly as an ethnic boundary marker? Does Augustine's account of the Trinity stand in opposition to cotemporary social Trinitarian accounts? (Or even: Does Eugene TeSelle's account of Augustine's account of the Trinity stand in opposition to contemporary social Trinitarian accounts? Or even further: Does Hiestand's account of TeSell's account of Augustine's account of the Trinity stand in opposition to contemporary social Trinitarian accounts? And on it goes). All are valid and important questions. But in each example, the underlying pastoral stakes are not made explicit.

Insofar as the ecclesial theologian self-consciously and vocationally identifies as a pastor, his writing at the outset makes explicit the pastoral questions that shape his overall project. This prioritization of ecclesial concerns then serves as a stated organizing principle for the ecclesial theologian's scholarship.[4] The ecclesial theologian thus offers more than a few

---

4. Compare, for example, John Lawson and Eric Osborne in their respective books on Irenaeus: John Lawson, *The Biblical Theology of Saint Irenaeus* (Eugene, Ore.: Wipf & Stock, 1948), and Eric Osborne, *Irenaeus of Lyon* (Cambridge: Cambridge University Press, 2001). Lawson wrote the bulk of his book while serving as a rural cleric among the villages of Colsterworth,

introductory pastoral comments at the outset of his project. Rather, he offers a detailed account of exactly how and why it is worth the church's time to study Athanasius's anthropology, Thomas's account of free will, Melanchthon's articulation of justification, Barth's epistemology, etc. The ecclesial theologian frames up, in very clear terms, the ecclesial stakes of the project. Likewise, the ecclesial theologian concludes his project with a clear appropriation of the subject analyzed with a view to deepening the health and faith of God's people. This appropriating impulse is not merely an appendix—not a few brief reflections tacked on the end of an otherwise completed project. Rather, the whole project is framed in a way that requires a pastoral conclusion.[5]

At root, an ecclesial theologian is not interested in Justin or Dunn or Augustine for the sake of mere intellectual curiosity (nor, of course, are good academic theologians). Ecclesial theologians approach theological scholarship in hopes that their findings will deepen the integrity of the church, inspire faith, and birth in the Christian a love for God and others. *These* are the topics that shape his theological scholarship. As such, the ecclesial theologian does not write about Justin or Dunn or Augustine *per se*. Rather, the ecclesial theologian writes about Christian witness in the face of pagan hostility and looks to Justin insofar as Justin informs that witness; or he writes about human efforts at self-justification and, as a consequence, notes how Dunn's account of first-century Judaism helps us (or doesn't help us) live faithfully in light of God's call; or, wishing to say something helpful about the importance of Christian community, he might look to Augustine's account of the Trinity. In other words, it is the pastoral consideration that frames and organizes the work of the ecclesial theologian.

Lincolnshire, and the pastoral impulses in his work are evident throughout. What's more, he makes the pastoral concern of his project—the unity of the Church—explicit in the introduction. Noting the import of Irenaeus for modern discussions regarding Catholicity and Christian unity, Lawson writes, "May the present study contribute some small thing to the advancement of that day for which we pray when we show forth the Lord's death, the day in which 'all they that do confess Thy holy Name may agree in the truth of Thy holy Word, and life in unity and godly love.'" Osborne, on the other hand, a university professor, offers us no such pastoral orientation in the preface of his work; instead, we find the sorts of things that (understandably) matter in the academic context: a brief overview of Irenaeus's themes, a preliminary assessment of recent scholarship, a few clarifying remarks regarding methodology, and so forth. Osborne's approach, while not without merit, minimizes any effort to appropriate Irenaeus as a contemporary theological or ecclesial resource. Osborne's approach is typical in academic scholarship.

5. A good example here is John Piper's response to N. T. Wright. See the introductory chapter of his *The Future of Justification: A Response to N. T. Wright* (Wheaton, Ill., Crossway, 2007). Whatever one might think about Piper's conclusion, certainly his pastoral and ecclesial concerns are made explicit in a way that is seldom seen in academic works on the same topic.

3. The Ecclesial Theologian Aims
for Clarity over Subtlety

Third, the ecclesial theologian, given the pastoral *telos* of his project, will tend to move from complexity to simplicity rather than the reverse. This is in contrast to much academic theology. The academic theologian feels, ever looming on the defensive perimeters of his theological scholarship, the assaults (both potential and actual) of his academic peers. Forestalling such assaults often pushes his scholarship into layers of qualifying and complexity that are perhaps necessary but often counterproductive with respect to usefulness. But the ecclesial theologian looks to simplify complex discussions toward a pastoral and missional outcome. As such, the ecclesial theologian is less concerned with forestalling potential critiques by other scholars (though he cannot be wholly free of this concern) and is more concerned with clarifying and articulating the church's message.

Here, an instructive comparison can be made between Karl Barth and Eduard Thurneysen. Barth and Thurneysen were close personal friends, Barth serving in the academy, Thurneysen serving in the church. Barth's contributions to contemporary theology are well-known. Yet Thurneysen was a genuine scholar and theologian in his own right. His shorter work *Dostoevsky* and his *The Sermon on the Mount* both reveal the range of his interests and the depth of his theological insight. And his *A Theology of Pastoral Care* offers a profoundly rich approach to pastoral ministry.[6] Throughout their respective careers, Barth and Thurneysen readily acknowledged their theological indebtedness to each other, such that they could "without any loss of integrity, take almost complete responsibility for the conclusions of the other."[7] They came to share a common theological vision, with Barth going so far as to say that his vision for a theology focused on God's revelation of himself through Scripture was first introduced to him by Thurneysen.

Yet in spite of their nearly identical theological perspectives, the difference of their respective social locations can be felt in the tone of their scholarship. Above all, Thurneysen writes as a pastor, with a simplicity

---

6. See his *Dostoevsky* (Eugene, Ore.: Wipf & Stock, 1963); *The Sermon on the Mount* (Eugene, Ore.: Wipf & Stock, 1963); *A Theology of Pastoral Care* (Eugene, Ore.: Wipf & Stock, 1962). Beyond a number of German works on a wide range of theological issues, the English reader will also find instructive a number of Thurneysen's sermons (published along with Barth). See *Come, Holy Spirit: Sermons* (New York: Round Table Press, 1933).

7. James D. Smart, "Eduard Thurneysen: Pastor Theologian," *Theology Today*, vol. 16 (1959): 77.

and pastoral directness that Barth lacks. James D. Smart, writing of the differences between the two, states, "Barth is so aware of the possibility of being misunderstood that he conditions each statement first against misinterpretations on the right and then against misinterpretations on the left, with the consequence that the whole appears tortured and so involved that even theologians become lost at times in the complications and fail to grasp the importance of the distinctions. But Thurneysen's style is more straightforward, with a simplicity and vividness of statement that make it eminently readable."[8] Throughout his work, Thurneysen demonstrates a robust grasp of his contemporary theological discussion partners. But his work does not show a preoccupation with the secondary literature or an acute need to forestall the critiques of other scholars. The ecclesial theologian, like Thurneysen, is concerned to clarify the gospel for the sake of the church.

4. The Ecclesial Theologian Theologizes with a Preaching Voice

Insofar as the ecclesial theologian writes as a pastor, the ecclesial theologian is not afraid to preach through his theology. Here again, we contrast the ecclesial theologian with a stereotype of the academic theologian. Academic theology does not generally get preachy. There are exceptions, of course.[9] But on the whole, the academy prioritizes disinterested neutrality and frowns upon the sort of dramatics one finds in a Luther or the explicit pietistic concerns of a Wesley. But the ecclesial theologian does not remove the clerical vestment when he takes up the pen. The pulpit is always in view, even if indirectly. Certainly, each pastor is different, and thus each pastor's written "preaching voice" will be different. But nonetheless, the ecclesial theologian carries the preacher's burden into his scholarship, resulting in earnest admonitions toward repentance, faith in Christ, love of God and neighbor, and personal holiness. Orthopraxy and doxology—not mere clarity—is the goal of the ecclesial theologian. As such, the ecclesial theologian's scholarship should call for both.

---

8. Smart, "Eduard Thurneysen," 81. For more on the relationship between Barth and Thurneysen, see the whole essay.

9. One thinks here of David Wells as a ready example of an academic theologian who often gets preachy. Of course, whether our assessment of Wells as "preachy" is a compliment or a critique will depend on one's social location. We intend it as a compliment.

John Webster helpfully illustrates this point in his treatment of Bonhoeffer's evolution from an academic theologian to ecclesial theologian.[10] Webster notes that Bonhoeffer moves from an interest in metaphysics (as seen in his *Sanctorum Communio* and *Act and Being*) to a preoccupation with exhortation in his biblical writings. "To read the biblical writings from the 1930s is not to be invited to reflect, but to be summoned by evangelical address."[11] And again, "The direct, homiletical rhetoric, the deliberate avoidance of technicality or complexity, the prose stripped to the basics, are all tokens of the fact that Bonhoeffer has come round to an understanding of the task of interpreting Scripture which is governed by two convictions: that the Holy Scripture is the *viva vox Dei*, and that this living voice demands an attitude of ready submission and active compliance."[12]

Like Bonhoeffer after 1930, the ecclesial theologian is not content to speak in theory or in disinterested tones but presses beyond theological theory and logical analysis toward God's prophetic call upon the lives of his people.

5. The Ecclesial Theologian Is a Student of the Church

The ecclesial theologian is a theologian of the church, for the church. As such, the ecclesial theologian is a student of the church—not only of her present resources, but also of the wealth of resources housed within her tradition. Remembering and drawing from this treasure room is a chief characteristic of the ecclesial theologian.

The needs of humanity in any given age circle back on the same basic questions—who am I? Who are you? Who is God? Who am I in relation to God, to you, to my world? What is my future? What do I exist for? Despite the remarkable changes to human life over the past hundred years, human ontology remains the same. As the Preacher has said, "There is nothing new under the sun." It is this continuity of the human condition

---

10. John Webster, *Word and Church: Essays in Christian Dogmatics* (New York: T&T Clark, 2001), 99. The terms *academic* and *ecclesial* here do not speak to Bonhoeffer's profession, but rather his identity as a theologian. In the 1930s, Bonhoeffer began to identify less with the academy and more with the church.

11. Ibid., 99.

12. Ibid., 101.

that makes the theological resources of the past worth investigating. While Athanasius was not confronted by the misguided anthropology of Cartesian mind-body dualism, he was confronted by Arianism. And the Christology and subsequent anthropology that emerged out of this fourth-century controversy offers the contemporary church theological resources for thinking about what it means to be human today. As such, the ecclesial theologian is well-read in the sweep of the church's literature and draws from the Christian tradition's most enduring works — Scripture not least.

Too often evangelicals — perhaps given our activist heritage — have lost sight of Catholic tradition and our part in it. And when we do reach into the past, we very frequently stop at the sixteenth century (and from there, we make our own Harnackian leap back to the apostles). Yet just as we stand in need of contemporary dialog partners, so too we stand in need of historic dialog partners.

The work of Richard Lovelace embodies this ideal. Lovelace is a Princeton-educated historian who taught for many years at Gordon-Conwell Theological Seminary. In his seminal work, *Dynamics of Spiritual Life*, Lovelace seeks to "isolate the main streams of spiritual vitality which have flowed through the church's history and to determine the principles which govern the force of these."[13] Toward this end, Lovelace offers a theory of spiritual renewal that draws not only from the Reformed tradition, but from the Anabaptist, pietistic, neo-Pentecostal, and Roman Catholic traditions as well. His work highlights two important ideals of the ecclesial theologian: it is driven by explicitly Christian concerns (i.e., how to bring about spiritual renewal), and it taps the wealth of the church throughout its history. Though a committed evangelical, Lovelace does not limit himself to an examination of the evangelical tradition alone.

It is either ignorance or hubris (or some combination of the two) that causes us to neglect the theological scholarship of the past. The ecclesial theologian does not forget that he is a theologian of the church universal, nor does he forget that the church stands with unfurled banners on the timeline of history, offering the time-tested fruit of orthodoxy and orthopraxy. The ecclesial theologian respects this tradition and takes his place within it.

---

13. Richard F. Lovelace, *Dynamics of Spiritual Life: An Evangelical Theory of Renewal* (Downers Grove, Ill.: InterVarsity, 1979), 11–12.

6. The Ecclesial Theologian
Works across the Guilds

The contemporary fragmentation of religious studies into narrow and specialized guilds complicates the work of the ecclesial theologian.[14] Too often by today's standard, the integrity of a theologian's project is measured with respect to his mastery of a subject matter that is a narrow "postage-stamp-sized bailiwick."[15] But without generalist accounts, specialists lose their ability to adequately interpret their own narrow data against the backdrop of the whole; the forest is lost for the trees. This specialist standard of theological scholarship seriously hampers the work of theology proper—insofar as theology attempts to synthesize multiple data points.[16] Generalist accounts are necessary, and it is here that ecclesial theologians are best positioned to contribute.

Like their academic counterparts, ecclesial theologians have a focus, an area of expertise, be it Old Testament, New Testament, systematics, historical studies, sociology, or classics—and all the inevitable specialized focus that goes along with each of these scholarly guilds. But as a pastor, there is a need for the ecclesial theologian to broaden beyond any one particular area of expertise. By the necessity of his trade and the questions that press upon him, the ecclesial theologian must be more than a specialist. Consequently, the ecclesial theologian does not generally pursue the same sort of specialized and narrowly focused scholarship that is often prioritized in the academy. Narrow work in a specialized guild (textual criticism on extant copies of Gregory of Nyssa's *Contra Eunomius*, for instance), while important in our critical and postcritical context, is most likely not the best use of the pastoral social location.

Insofar as the narrow research focus of the modern PhD dissertation represents the benchmark of true scholarship, this far must the ecclesial theologian part ways with his academic counterpart. This is not to say that

14. For a detailed treatment of the fragmentation of theology post-Enlightenment, see Edward Farley's, *Theologia: The Fragmentation and Unity of Theological Education* (Eugene, Ore.: Wipf & Stock, 1994).

15. Markus Bockmuehl, *Seeing the Word: Refocusing New Testament Study* (Grand Rapids: Baker, 2007), 35.

16. The need for generalists is not only an ecclesial concern. In many of the academic guilds—biblical studies especially—the narrow specialization hampers constructive readings of the biblical text. In defense of generalists, see Michael Bird and Craig Keener, "Jack of All Trades, Master of None: The Case for Generalist Scholars in Biblical Scholarship," *SBL Forum* 7.4 (2009).

ecclesial theologians will never do narrow research in a particular guild. But it is to say that ecclesial theologians are less motivated to engage in narrow research and more motivated to synthesize and issue prophetic calls. What's more, they are well positioned to do so. Without the pressure of the academic guilds, ecclesial theologians have more freedom to engage in cross-guild projects that are explicitly generalist, and thus more readily theological and pastoral. The ecclesial theologian thus offers an important counterbalance to the reigning trend toward specialization in academic theology.

N. T. Wright is a positive example here. Wright was trained as a New Testament scholar—and an academic one at that. Yet his work, especially during his tenure in the church, was very often broadly theological and outside the academic New Testament guild. This can be seen in his work on the doctrine of justification, which moves beyond a narrow focus on Paul.[17] It is also evident in his biblical theology and eschatology. His book, *Surprised by Hope: Rethinking Heaven, the Resurrection, and the Mission of the Church* is distinctly pastoral and draws upon the full sweep of Scripture to construct a Christian eschatology meant to fuel right Christian living. The pastoral impulses and agenda are evident throughout.

Yet there are legitimate pitfalls that attend the generalist. If specialists miss the forest for the trees, generalists often miss the wonderful diversity of the trees within the forest. This leads to our seventh characteristic of the ecclesial theologian: the ecclesial theologian works in partnership with the academic theologian.

7. The Ecclesial Theologian Works in Partnership with the Academic Theologian

The university remains the intellectual center of Western culture, and North American culture not least. The retreatist mindset of nineteenth-century Christianity—as seen in both the Protestant and Catholic responses to modernity—did much damage to the cause of Christ in North America.[18] Christianity cannot cede a "faithful presence" (to borrow James

---

17. See especially his *Justification: God's Plan and Paul's Vision* (Downers Grove, Ill.: InterVarsity, 2009).

18. For the best retelling of the North American narrative, see Mark Noll's, *The Scandal of the Evangelical Mind* (Grand Rapids: Eerdmans, 1994), as well as George Marsden, *The Soul of the American University: From Protestant Establishment to Established Nonbelief* (Oxford: Oxford University Press, 1994).

Hunter's term) in the intellectual center of contemporary culture and hope to advance the supremacy of Christ in all facets of life. A Christian witness that cannot engage with the intellectual elites of a culture is a Christian witness doomed to irrelevance, no matter how fervent its piety. As such, we readily acknowledge and cheerlead for the importance of evangelicals within the secular universities. But beyond this "missionary" value, ecclesial theologians stand in need of the sort of work at which the academy is so adept. Far from going it alone, the ecclesial theologian recognizes that the resources of the academy are vital to the work of ecclesial theology. Partnership is needed in at least two ways.

First, the ecclesial theologian needs the specialized resourcing of the academy. At the close of the 2009 symposium on the "Identity of the Pastor Theologian" hosted by the Center for Pastor Theologians, Douglas Sweeney, professor of church history at Trinity Evangelical Divinity School, offered the following proposal regarding a possible working relationship between academic scholars and a new generation of ecclesial theologians:

> We are not often explicit about this, but systematic theology, insofar as it is distinguished from biblical, historical, philosophical, psychological, and intercultural theology, is the work of generalists.... They put the big picture together and apply it to our lives.... In fact, the people best suited to synthesize our knowledge of God and His ways in the world, applying this knowledge to the empirical realities people face, are pastor theologians.
>
> We should work toward a day when professors view themselves as handmaids serving pastor theologians, and pastor theologians play an important public role in guiding people theologically. Professors should continue to offer specialized instruction in ancient languages and history, exegesis, church history, social science, and philosophy. They will continue to raise up future generations of pastors. But we should work to raise up the kinds of pastors who can synthesize, exposit, and apply the knowledge of God to the lives of all God's people with authority.[19]

Sweeney's comments helpfully delineate the respective strengths of both the academy and the church. The pastoral office is capable of theological scholarship, and we serve the church poorly when we forget this. Yet ecclesial theologians, even working as generalists, need to draw upon the specialized work done by academic scholars. The academic vocation

---

19. Douglas A. Sweeney, "Sixteen Theses on the Pastor Theologian," presented at the annual gathering of the Center for Pastor Theologians, October, 2009.

offers the academic research professor time and resources that the ecclesial theologian will not be able to match. When functioning in service of the church, the ability of an academic scholar to produce technical work that drills deeply into a narrow focus is a great value to Christian theology and a tremendous resource for ecclesial theologians.

Given the rise of the modern research university, as well as the development of the specialized guilds, it is not realistic (at least for the foreseeable future) to expect ecclesial theologians to flourish wholly independent of the academy. The fields have simply become too specialized and the secondary literature too vast. Likewise, the church does not have the institutional structures in place to facilitate the sort of specialized research that now takes place in the academy. Notably, nearly all the learned societies are distinctly academic.

Second, beyond resourcing ecclesial theologians, the prioritization of objectivity and neutrality within the academy helps to keep the ecclesial theologian honest. In a (perhaps overreaching) characterization, academic theologians tend to work from theory to praxis. This is not to say that academic theologians always fail to arrive at praxis, only that they do not begin there, nor does praxis shape the contours of their work in the same way that one more naturally finds in the work of an ecclesial theologian. At first blush, this might be seen as a weakness of academic theology. And in one sense, it is. But in another sense, the academic focus on theory enables the academic theologian to ferret out the philosophical shortcomings of a given paradigm, in ways that ecclesial theologians may not be as careful to do.

Academic theologians, inasmuch as they are not driven by praxis to the same degree as ecclesial theologians, more naturally engage with the merit of an idea *as an idea* and not as a means of changing behavior. The ecclesial theologian's temptation to simplify and apply can, if one isn't carful, lead to reductionism or overreaching conclusions. The academic theologian's movement from theory to praxis provides a valuable check to the pastor theologian's sense of ecclesial urgency.

8. The Ecclesial Theologian Traffics in Introspection

Much of the hard work of the theologian is to peel back the layers of surface-level, stated belief that mask the underlying core beliefs and then to reshape these core beliefs in ways consistent with the gospel. And it is here that ecclesial theologians have a unique and vital role to play in the theological and ethical formation of God's people. The ecclesial theologian studies the self as much as he studies the work of other theologians. He becomes a master of the interior, a physician of the soul and its motivations. He mines deeply beneath the surface, moving beyond the conscious and stated reasons for behavior, and locates the core convictions that give birth to human desires and will. Academic theologians can do this too, of course. But the academic guild, as a matter of practice, does not generally leave room for this type of introspective theology.

Augustine most readily comes to mind at this point. Augustine's *Confessions*, chief among his voluminous works, delves deeply into the human psyche. In this autobiographical work, Augustine is keen to understand why he does what he does. Why did he steal those peaches as a young man? Why is he so drawn to friendship and companionship? What is it about sex that so captivates him and tempts him toward idolatry? Why does he let himself daydream about a hound chasing a hare when he should be praying? Augustine is not content to simply issue imperatives (to himself or others). He yearns to understand himself so that he might better direct his heart and the hearts of those he is called to shepherd, toward God. He sees the vital link between thought and action, between belief and love. It is because Augustine has come to understand himself so thoroughly that he is so able to direct us out of the labyrinths of our own misplaced loves and vain idolatry.

Following in the steps of Augustine requires longer legs than most of us have. Yet Augustine's example on this point provides a useful ideal for ecclesial theologians and points Christian theology in a direction that is neglected at present.

Conclusion

In a very real way, questions about the sort of project an ecclesial theologian might engage in is ultimately answered by the sort of project an ecclesial theologian actually *does* engage in. Or to say it again, the best way to define the theological project of an ecclesial theologian is to look at the work of ecclesial theologians. But this is difficult to do in our contemporary context. Given that the paradigm has largely died, the best we can do is point pastors in the sort of directions we ourselves are inclined to go.

As such, we do not here presume to have spoken the final word regarding the identity of the ecclesial theologian or his work. Insofar as we are attempting to bring forward an ancient paradigm into a modern age, we readily acknowledge that our identification of the ecclesial theologian is a work in progress. The work of actual ecclesial theologians may very likely take shape in ways we have not anticipated. No doubt a future generation of ecclesial theologians will be better positioned to offer a more realistic account. But a preliminary account is necessary nonetheless, and we have offered it here in hopes of generating initial momentum for the vision.

Not every pastor is gifted or called to be an ecclesial theologian, of course. But evangelicalism's future vision of the pastor theologian must include that of the ecclesial theologian, and this model of the theologian must serve as a viable and complimentary alternative to the academic theologian.

And thus, we restate the principle thesis of this book. There is need, we believe, to challenge the emerging generation of theologians to seriously consider the context of their theological calling. The church is in need of theologians who once again don the clerical mantle—who work explicitly and openly within the framework of historic, Nicene orthodoxy; who work and write as those who bear the weight of souls upon their shoulders; who write—above all—as *pastors*. Such writing has been the lifeblood of the church and has constituted her highest theological discourse. It is, we are convinced, only by reuniting the office of pastor with the historic duty of the theologian that evangelicalism can begin to address the theological anemia of the church and the ecclesial anemia of theology.

Yet moving forward in this direction will be a challenge. In our next chapter, we offer ten steps for living out the vocation of an ecclesial theologian in a local church context.

CHAPTER 8

On Being an Ecclesial Theologian in a Local Church

I get up at 4:30 a.m.   *Peter Liethart*

Today, there are very few ecclesial theologians in churches. In previous chapters, we traced some of the historical and cultural reasons for this. Here, we turn to some of the practical reasons, which could be summarized bluntly as follows: it's hard to be an ecclesial theologian in a local church. That's not whining; that's reality.

For starters, there is little institutional support for ecclesial theologians. Nearly all the currents in the academy and the church push aspiring ecclesial theologians in a different direction, whether to do more "rigorous" or "academic" scholarship, or to be less "heady" and more "practical" in ministry. Frankly, this creates an inhospitable environment for ecclesial theologians, a state of affairs that is unlikely to change any time soon.

Of course, we need not overplay the challenges of our contemporary context, as though ours is the first age in the history of the church when pastors struggled to be theologians. If we read the letters of Augustine, perhaps the greatest of the ecclesial theologians, we see the tension is as old as the pastoral vocation itself. We know the great nineteenth-century German biblical theologian Adolf Schlatter spent the early part of his life in parish ministry and found it difficult to sustain serious theological labor while carrying out his ministerial duties, something he lamented to his friend Adolf Bollinger.[1] Or more recently, we see renowned New Testament scholar N. T. Wright feeling compelled to resign his bishopric to create more space for scholarly pursuits.[2] Evidently, the calling of ecclesial theologians isn't for the faint of heart!

Despite the challenges, however, it is possible to be an ecclesial

---

1. See Werner Neuer, *Adolf Schlatter: A Biography of Germany's Premier Biblical Theologian*, trans. Robert W. Yarbrough (Grand Rapids: Baker, 1995), 63.

2. See chapter 2 for more on N. T. Wright's decision to resign as Bishop of Durham to assume a teaching post at the University of St. Andrews, Scotland.

theologian. But to do so requires thoughtfulness and intentionality; it won't just happen. In fact, pastors in pursuit of this calling need to adopt a few well-conceived strategies and take some bold and creative steps to see it happen. The aim of this chapter is to offer that kind of practical advice. Drawing on our own experience, we offer ten strategies to help pastors pursue the vision of being an ecclesial theologian in a local church.

Perhaps we should add that when it comes to being an ecclesial theologian, there is no silver bullet. At least, we've not found one. Nor to our knowledge is there some secret formula for mixing up the perfect batch of ecclesial theologians, hidden away in some vault in Wheaton or Grand Rapids. We also do not presume to be the perfect models of ecclesial theologians; in reality, the counsel we offer here is borne out of our experience of slogging it out in our church, with all the attendant fits and starts, successes and setbacks, victories and frustrations. In short, we have not yet arrived; we're only pilgrims along the way.

To better appreciate the strategies set forth in this chapter, a word about our own ecclesial setting would be helpful. Our church is located in the heart of Oak Park, Illinois, the nearest western suburb of Chicago. It is an affluent urban-suburban community adjacent to one of Chicago's poorest and most crime-ridden neighborhoods. We have an average weekly attendance of seven hundred adults, with lots of babies and kids to boot. We have eight ministry staff (a mix of part-time and full-time), plus an equivalent number of support staff. Todd is the senior pastor and shoulders the responsibility for preaching and vision; Gerald is the senior associate pastor and focuses on discipleship and staff management. Our church is diverse with respect to background, race, age, and socioeconomic status.

Of course, much of what we say has been worked out in this particular context, and insofar as others serve in different settings, there will need to be a certain amount of adapting and transposing of what we say. In addition, we've written this chapter to help seminarians and postgraduates who are preparing for ministry; our desire is that they will find some helpful insights they can put into practice now so as to facilitate their transition into ministry and their pursuit of the vision of a being an ecclesial theologian.

Finally, given the diversity of ecclesial settings, we've included three case studies from pastoral colleagues and fellow members of the Center for Pastor Theologians who serve in very different settings. After providing a brief introductory biography, we then ask them to speak about the challenges to and practical steps for realizing the vision of being an ecclesial theologian.

Strategy One: Get a PhD[3]

We begin with this not because it is the most important strategy, but because it is a critical part of the *preparation* we believe is necessary for ecclesial theologians. The costs of a PhD — financial, emotional, familial — are significant and not to be taken lightly. For some, a PhD may not be possible or prudent. Yet those who aspire to be ecclesial theologians should think seriously about pursuing a PhD. True, Karl Barth didn't have a PhD. But until you've written something remotely akin to his *Römerbrief*, you should probably get on with getting one; it will almost certainly be necessary for pursuing the sort of vision we've laid out for the ecclesial theologian. We say this for at least three reasons.

1. *Training.* The PhD offers a regimen of disciplined training that would be very difficult to get independently. Despite the limitations of social location, academic scholars know their business, namely, research. The task of the ecclesial theologian will likely be less focused research than that of an academic scholar; yet locating and properly handling primary and secondary sources is vital to the work of the ecclesial theologian, and academic theologians are best positioned to provide tutelage in this area. To be sure, the theological method of the academy is not always congruous with the theological method we envision for the ecclesial theologian. And in this sense, pursuing a PhD as training for becoming an ecclesial theologian may be a bit like a long-distance runner training for a triathlon; it won't be an exact match. But at present, the academy is still the best training out there for acquiring the sort of research competency we envision being necessary for ecclesial theologians. This competency and experience can be accomplished in limited measures through an MA or an MDiv; but anyone who has done a PhD will tell you that the requirements of a postgraduate research degree push beyond anything seen at a graduate level.

2. *Networking.* Working on a PhD will broaden your network of relationships with other thinkers and scholars, particularly with academic theologians. In keeping with our comments in the previous chapter, your ongoing work as an ecclesial theologian will need to be carried out in partnership with academic theologians. Involvement in a PhD program helps to establish relationships with other scholars — both ecclesial and academic — and connects you to networks that won't otherwise be

---

3. Some of the content for this chapter is drawn from a short piece Gerald wrote for Kevin Vanhoozer and Owen Strachan's *The Pastor as Public Theologian: Reclaiming a Lost Vision* (Grand Rapids: Brazos, 2015).

accessible. As a pastor doing theology, these relationships and networks are vital, insofar as they are no longer readily available in your pastoral vocation.

3. *Publishing.* The PhD remains the intellectual's best calling card. Resist it as a pretentious, elitist social construct, but there it is all the same. And truthfully, a PhD demonstrates that one has at least a modicum of intellectual firepower, as well as the work ethic necessary to see a serious intellectual undertaking all the way through to completion. There are other intellectual calling cards, of course, but a PhD will help open doors for you in terms of scholarship and publication that would otherwise require more vigorous knocking. This is not to say that publishers will certainly look at your manuscript because you have a PhD or that they will certainly reject your book proposals because you don't. But it is to say that having a reputable PhD at least earns you the benefit of the doubt. This is all the more important given the fact that your vocation as a pastor will bring with it assumptions about your intellectual caliber that may tend in the opposite direction.

But once you've decided to get a PhD, you'll find that the road forks in further directions. Do you pursue a taught program or a research program? Full time or part time? Residency or nonresidency?

What Kind of PhD: Taught or Research? Residency or Nonresidency?

There are two types of PhD programs: taught programs and research programs. For the uninitiated, a taught program requires coursework plus a dissertation. A research program tends only to require a dissertation. Most divinity schools and universities in the United States offer taught programs; most in the United Kingdom offer research programs (with some taught components). The primary advantage of a research program is that it allows for a "deep dive" in a narrow topic, thus enabling the student to focus complete attention on an area of research. The advantage of the taught program is that it is well rounded and forces the student to acquire a wider range of competency than is typically found in research programs. It is generally agreed that those seeking a teaching position (as opposed to a research position) in an academic context are best prepared through a taught program. Because the ecclesial theologian tends to be a generalist rather than a specialist, such programs could offer very effective preparation.

Yet those already serving in pastoral ministry (here we have in mind primarily North American pastors), or who do not have the resources to sustain a full-time taught program, may want to look closely at a nonresidency research program.[4] Such programs can be done either part-time or full-time. A significant advantage of a part-time nonresidency research program is that it allows you to stay grounded in an ecclesial context while you engage in your research. The academic pressure to subordinate your ecclesial impulses is lessened when one writes a dissertation with a certain amount of remove from the social location of the academy. If you are situated in a church context that is willing to give you a couple of mornings a week to study and write, and you have access to a good research library, this may be your best bet. But there are challenges to a part-time nonresidency program. Heed them well, and then proceed with caution.

First, a nonresidency degree requires a significant level of self-motivation. The distractions of life and ministry will have a tendency to serve as speed bumps in your research, if not roadblocks altogether. If you are the sort of person who gets distracted easily, and who thrives on a high amount of relational encouragement and accountability, a residency program may be a better route for you.

Second, supervision of nonresidency programs can be hit or miss. Many nonresidency doctoral candidates complain that their supervisors are inaccessible and unresponsive. This isn't always the case, of course, but you'll want to be sure you locate a supervisor who has a positive track record supervising distance students. If executed well, Skype, email, and the occasional personal visit are effective methods of supervision. But nothing is worse than spending precious time and money on a degree and getting little or no help from your supervisor.

Finally, a nonresidency program will not result in the same level of networking that one finds in a residency program. For the most part, you will hover around the margins of the intellectual life and social networks of your university. The various seminars and informal meetings among the PhD students of your university will be largely inaccessible. Insofar as one of the primary benefits of a PhD program is building a network, this is a significant shortcoming.

---

4. The major UK schools such as Cambridge and Oxford generally have residency requirements for both their taught and research programs. But in many universities (St. Andrews, Kent, etc.), residency requirements are established through the schools/colleges that compose the university rather than by the university itself. So, ultimately, you'll need to check with the school or college to be sure about their residency requirements.

But having offered the above disclaimers, if you have the sort of personality that can steadily plod along, and you have access to a good library, a nonresidency program can work well. When factored together with one's family responsibilities, ministry commitments, and financial realities, a nonresidency degree may be your best (or perhaps only!) option.

Strategy Two: Staff to the Vision

Building a staff that values theology will go a long way toward creating a robust theological culture at your church. To be sure, there may be many in your church who appreciate the work you do as a theologian, even if they don't fully understand it. But in many respects, this is like the doctor being appreciated by his patients; the appreciation is valued, but it does not help to deepen the doctor's own sense of vocational calling or medical competency. Insofar as theological scholarship is best done in community, the ecclesial theologian will benefit from serving alongside a like-minded colleague.

We (the authors) serve together in a multistaff church. The mutual and regular exchange with respect to our various projects goes a long way toward keeping us both diligent in staying after the ecclesial-theologian vision. Beyond this, we have been able to gather together a number of other thoughtful pastors. All of this has been a tremendous help in creating an overall staff culture that appreciates and encourages theological scholarship. In our previous church contexts, we didn't have a working environment where we could pop our head into the study next door and talk about how Aquinas's prioritization of the intellect helped him arrive at a different *ordo salutis* than Calvin, and the implications this has for the doctrine of total depravity. But now we do. And the difference it has made is significant for ongoing theological reflection. If you can add to your church staff a like-minded partner who is serious about theological scholarship, you will have gone a long way in overcoming a major hurdle for the ecclesial theologian: isolation.

Keep in mind, however, that we pastor-theologian types do have our blind spots. There is more to leading a healthy church than providing theological depth. As such, we are not suggesting pastors of multistaff churches hire only pastor theologians. The church needs the full range of gifts; so, yes, hire pastors with gifts in counseling, leadership, evangelism, and administration. But do hire, if at all possible, at least one like-minded colleague. It will make a world of difference.

Strategy Three: Get Networked

Not all of us are in a position to hire a fellow ecclesial theologian, or even another local theologian. Perhaps you're a solo pastor in a smaller congregation, or you don't oversee the hiring process. Regardless, you can engage in or develop a network of like-minded pastoral colleagues. For some, this is found at denominational meetings; for others, it consists of informal gatherings of pastors in your area. Either way, it is crucial to lock arms with colleagues who are pursuing the ecclesial theologian vision with you. In addition, these networks open doors to publishing opportunities, stimulate ideas for research, provide access to resources, and give much-needed encouragement.[5]

Meeting together in person is most effective, but digital meetings can work well. Gerald meets monthly with two other pastors via Skype to discuss what they have been reading and writing. Each pastor takes a turn presenting the latest draft of a writing project, and the others offer feedback. These regular exchanges help provide camaraderie and motivation in the often arduous task of writing. Regardless, then, of the shape it takes for you, find other pastors who are committed to theological scholarship, and establish a regular pattern of meetings. You will be the better for it.

In addition to networking with other ecclesial theologians, develop relationships with academic theologians who love the church and are sympathetic to the vision of the ecclesial theologian. At present, academic theologians are best positioned to provide resourcing to help with many aspects of your scholarly work. They occupy a different world, to be sure. And their theological focus may not always point in the same direction as yours. But there is simply no way for an ecclesial theologian to do his job at a distance from the resources of the academy. So grab coffee with the local seminary faculty member, or strike up an email conversation with the theologian whose book you just finished reading. Be proactive, and you will find a surprising number of doors open to you.

---

5. Toward this end, the Center for Pastor Theologians will begin (in the Fall of 2015) hosting an annual theology conference in Chicago. We intend this to be a way for like-minded folks to gather together and begin to form thick networks. For more information about the CPT's theology conference, visit us online at www.pastortheologians.com.

Case Study: Michael LeFebvre

Dr. Michael LeFebvre is the pastor of Christ Church Reformed Presbyterian in Brownsburg, Indiana. Christ Church is a recent church plant organized in 2006 by the Reformed Presbyterian Church of North America (RPCNA). The church has around eighty members, with three ruling elders and no staff apart from the pastor. The congregation currently meets in rented space in the western suburbs of Indianapolis and draws its members from throughout the Indianapolis metropolitan area. Michael earned his PhD in Old Testament from the University of Aberdeen in 2005. His dissertation was on the reception of the Mosaic law-writings in the Second Temple period (published as *Collections, Codes, and Torah: The Re-characterization of Israel's Written Law*; LHBOTS 451[T&T Clark, 2006]). Michael has written numerous books, including *Our Triune God: Living in the Love of the Three-in-One* (Crossway, 2011), and *The Gospel and Sexual Orientation* (Crown and Covenant, 2012).

In the following paragraphs, we will allow Dr. LeFebvre to respond to questions about his pastor-theologian experience.

What Are Your Greatest Challenges as You Seek to Embody the Ecclesial-Theologian Vision?

"It will come as no surprise that the greatest challenge I face is working within the constraints of limited time. As a husband and a father of five; the lone pastor, preacher, and administrator for my congregation; and with various roles within my presbytery and at the synod level of my denomination: managing my time for faithfulness in these realms while remaining steadfast in my continuing research and writing goals is a great challenge. But it is a challenge I welcome. I approach time management as a puzzle to solve week by week, looking for creative solutions each week to keep the plates spinning and to advance various needs and pursuits. And I have been an early riser since my teens, so I am used to getting up and starting each day early in order to maximize my productivity.

"Thankfully, I have enjoyed tremendous support for my theological pursuits from my family, my peers in the ministry, and my congregation. Serving in a denomination that retains an appreciation for robust theology is a great blessing. So I have experienced no challenges (and much encouragement) in my research and writing commitments from those among whom I serve."

What Are a Few Practical Steps You Have Found Helpful in Realizing the Vision of the Ecclesial Theologian?

"Access to scholarly resources is vital. One of my goals when pursuing a pastoral call was to find a pastorate in close proximity to a theological library. The presence of a seminary library in Indianapolis with lending privileges for area clergy was one factor contributing to my eagerness to accept my present position. I also retain a subscription to ATLA Serials online (which is available at a clergy rate through EBSCO), and the University of Aberdeen provides JSTOR access for alumni. The interlibrary loan service of my local public library has also been useful for obtaining titles not available through the aforementioned avenues. Setting up convenient access to scholarly resources (in addition to my personal library) has been extremely important for my work.

"I also believe it important to prioritize care for the local congregation above my research and writing projects. I strive to be a 'pastor theologian,' with pastor first for a reason. I would regard it far better, at the end of my life, to look back on only a few meaningful publications and a life of faithfully nurturing people, than to publish a mountain of important works at the expense of the sheep to which I am called. It is vital, in my view, to set aside the American idols of productivity and significance and instead to pray for contentment, faithfulness, and Christlike love.

"It is also helpful to multiply the usefulness of research hours whenever possible. Often, a sermon series I am preaching for the benefit of my congregation will overlap with areas of research I am pursuing. Making the most of those overlaps allows me to spend time in research that will have a payoff in both preaching and writing. However, my own research interests are primarily in the realm of biblical studies, so such overlap is more frequent for me than it might be for someone focused on, say, historical theology or systematics."

Strategy Four: Guard Your Study Time with a Blowtorch

When Todd was completing his doctoral studies and preparing to return to the States to take up a pastorate, he got to chatting with one of his mentoring professors who expressed some doubt about Todd's ability to maintain a research profile as a pastor. Todd, admittedly rather naively at the time, pushed back on the suggestion, to which the professor, not interested in debating the point, simply gave this piece of blunt advice: "Well, then, you'll need to guard your study time with a blowtorch."

Guarding your study time with a blowtorch may at first blush sound selfish, and admittedly it can degenerate into that. But for an ecclesial theologian, it can also be a means of survival, a way of staying true to what you believe the Lord has called you to do for the good of his church. John Stott would go to the Hookses, a study retreat on the coast of Wales, for a week or more to give himself space from the demands of pastoring to devote himself to study and writing. Creating physical distance is one way to do it, but it's not the only way. Exercising discipline over your schedule and working with well-defined and communicated boundaries is another way.

The lifeblood of a pastor, whether your congregation realizes it or not, is a steady diet of rich theology, prayer, and Bible reading. So stop feeling guilty about spending an hour on some Tuesday afternoon digesting Calvin's *Institutes* or Athanasius's *On the Incarnation* or Augustine's *On the Trinity*. Whether he is an ecclesial theologian or not, theological study isn't something a pastor fits into his schedule when he's completed his pastoral duties; it is part and parcel of his pastoral duty. For the good of your congregation, and for the good of your own preaching and teaching and counseling and writing, do not neglect to feed yourself from the riches of the Christian tradition.

Despite the necessity of this kind of reflection, the expectations and demands of your congregation will pull you away from it. If you're going to get after it, you are going to have to make it a priority in your schedule. Generally, the work of an ecclesial theologian requires large blocks of undistracted times. We've found that setting aside the morning hours works best for us. The advantage of prioritizing our study time in the morning (instead of the afternoon) is that we can start as early as we want, and we tend to have a head that is less cluttered by the day's events. Peter Leithart was once asked how he managed to be such a prolific writer. He shrugged and said, "I get up at 4:30 a.m." That'll do it.

Gerald typically sets aside two mornings a week for study and writing. On most of these mornings, he is at his desk by 6:00 a.m. and works until noon. Typically, he works on research that is not directly related to a sermon or a lesson (though most of the material finds its way there eventually). If his schedule is light for a given week, he can occasionally add part or all of a third morning. Todd keeps a similar schedule: up early, devotional reading and prayer first thing, then research, writing, and sermon prep for the remainder of the morning, with administrative tasks and meetings for the afternoon. Of course, these are our routines; they aren't meant to be normative for anyone else. In fact, each person needs to find his own groove and what works best for him, given who he is.[6]

It is also important to be intentional about the kind of work culture you create (or help perpetuate) at your church. For the most part, we've created a staff culture in which we reserve meetings, appointments, and other administrative tasks for the afternoon. Of course, sometimes things come up that take away from study, like a church-related emergency, a family going through crisis, or a funeral. These are to be taken in stride and not viewed as nuisances or distractions, because they are the warp and woof of healthy pastoral ministry. But we have found that an undistracted morning is an ecclesial theologian's optimal base of operations.

Eugene Peterson, in his insightful and inspiring book *The Contemplative Pastor*, gives busy pastors some excellent advice on how to get unbusy—take hold of your appointment calendar. "It is more effective than a protective secretary; it is less expensive than a retreat house. It is the one thing everyone in our society accepts without cavil as authoritative."[7] Peterson tells of the week he scheduled a two-hour appointment with Fyodor Dostoevsky. Why should we not schedule similar appointments with Jonathan Edwards, Karl Barth, or John Chrysostom? "If there is no time to nurture these essentials, I become a busy pastor, harassed and anxious, a whining, compulsive Martha instead of a contemplative Mary."[8]

Of course, this works best when you can control your schedule. Most pastors can, but some serve in churches where your schedule is at the mercy of others. Even so, there are probably times in a week that are usually more open. Schedule your study time in these slots. And depending upon your church, and the amount of space you have to pursue theological scholarship during normal working hours, you may have to be more intentional about your nonworking hours. You'll get no sympathy here, however, if

---

6. Here, one would do well to consult the fascinating and helpful book by Mason Currey, *Daily Rituals: How Artists Work* (New York: Knopf, 2013), which presents short vignettes of the work routines and daily habits of more than 150 different creative types, from Franz Kafka and Jonathan Edwards, to Jean-Paul Sartre and Woody Allen. His advice in the Introduction is worth quoting, "A solid routine fosters a well-worn groove for one's mental energies and helps stave off the tyranny of moods" (xiv).

7. Eugene Peterson, *The Contemplative Pastor: Returning to the Art of Spiritual Direction* (Grand Rapids: Eerdmans, 1993), 31.

8. Ibid., 32.

you watch Netflix ten hours a week but complain you have no time to be an ecclesial theologian. At the end of the day, we make time for what is important, and if being an ecclesial theologian is a priority, you will find a way to schedule it.

Strategy Five: Read Ecclesial Theology (and Other Stuff)

If you want to write ecclesial theology, you need to read ecclesial theology. This is because ecclesial theology is its own genre: learned but not ponderous, thoughtful but not tedious, careful but not so overly qualified as to muffle any sense of pastoral urgency. The challenge, however, is that most ecclesial theologians have cut their scholarly teeth on academic theology during graduate school. But academic prose, though not without merit, is usually not the best genre for doing ecclesial theology. Ecclesial theology is prophetic, not just informative; it's pastoral, not just scholarly; it's prescriptive, not just descriptive; it's aimed at the heart, not just the head. This kind of writing is hard to find in today's leading academic journals or monograph series; instead, we need to read those theologians whose writings have shaped the church's knowledge of and love for God. Who might these be? Theologians like Augustine and Basil, Calvin and Luther, Wesley and Edwards, Bonhoeffer and Barth. You'll need to read other theological works as well, of course, including recent academic work. But you'll want to make sure you have a steady intake of ecclesial theology to help you stay in tune with the work you're called to do.

Pastor theologian and missiologist Lesslie Newbigin advised pastors to always be working on one "big book"—a substantive, thought-provoking piece of theology one consumes slowly over time.[9] Todd took this advice to heart several years ago and began reading Jonathan Edwards's masterwork on Christian spirituality, *Religious Affections*, a treasure trove of pastoral counsel and theological insight. As part of his morning routine, Todd would read a dozen pages of Edwards, lingering over his observations, pondering his insights. He continued this for several years, working his way through the book, cover to cover, half a dozen times. In fact, on the title page of his copy of the Yale edition, you'll find written in shades of blue ink, "1st reading, Sept.–Oct. 2009; 2nd reading, April 2010; 3rd

9. See Lesslie Newbigin, *"The Good Shepherd": Meditations on Christian Ministry in Today's World* (Grand Rapids: Eerdmans, 1977), 114.

and 4th reading, March–May 2011; 5th reading, Oct. 2011; 6th reading, March 2013." This discipline was invaluable in its own right, but it proved immensely beneficial during a difficult time in the life of the church. Besides this, Todd's study of Edwards's big book turned out to be an inspiration for a sermon series he preached on authentic Christianity, which found its way into a book entitled, *Real Christian: Bearing the Marks of Authentic Faith*.[10]

In addition to reading serious theology, you should also make a point of reading good literature. Pick up Charles Dickens or Fyodor Dostoevsky, John Milton or Jane Austen, Herman Melville or John Steinbeck. Read classics not only for their insight into human experience, but for their masterful handling of the English language.[11] Gerald keeps a work of literature on his nightstand and reads a few pages each evening; beyond the enjoyment of it, he's found this practice serves as a nice palette cleanser after consuming academic theology. Todd got carried away with this principle and wound up coauthoring a book on how clergy are portrayed in literature.[12]

There is also wisdom in seasoning your reading with books from other (secular) fields of study, whether biology or sociology, economics or history. This can be like adding a dash of salt to your meal. "Salt needs to be in food, and theology needs to be in contact with the secular. Have some secular interests of your own which you keep up and develop. Your theology will be kept fresh if you do so."[13] Todd, for example, has developed something of an avocation reading in the natural sciences, especially evolutionary biology, and Gerald enjoys delving into Civil War–era history. Not only can this satisfy an intellectual curiosity, it can broaden one's perspective on the world and bring other lines of inquiry into conversation with one's theology.

---

10. Todd Wilson, *Real Christian: Bearing the Marks of Authentic Faith* (Grand Rapids: Zondervan, 2014).

11. See the excellent book by Cornelius Plantinga Jr., *Reading for Preaching: The Preacher in Conversation with Storytellers, Biographers, Poets, and Journalists* (Grand Rapids: Eerdmans, 2013).

12. Leland Ryken, Philip Graham Ryken, and Todd Wilson, *Pastors in the Classics: Timeless Lessons on Life and Ministry from World Literature* (Grand Rapids: Baker, 2011).

13. Newbigin, *Good Shepherd*, 114.

Case Study: Jeremy Treat

Dr. Jeremy Treat is a teaching pastor at Reality LA in Los Angeles. Reality LA is a nondenominational church that was planted in 2006. The church averages around three thousand in attendance (the majority of which are in their twenties), with seven pastors, and thirty people on staff. The church gathers on Sundays in a public high school in Hollywood and draws members from throughout Los Angeles. He also serves as an adjunct professor at Biola University. Jeremy earned his PhD from Wheaton College in 2013. His dissertation focused on the relationship between the atoning death of Christ and the kingdom of God and was published as *The Crucified King: Atonement and Kingdom in Biblical and Systematic Theology* (Zondervan, 2014).

Here he responds to our questions.

What Are Your Greatest Challenges as You Seek to Embody the Ecclesial-Theologian Vision?

"The first challenge is balance. My primary responsibility is as a pastor, but I also teach a bit at Biola University, and I feel called to write. And all of these, of course, are subordinate to my roles as a child of God, a husband to my wife, and father of four kids (all age four and under). The key for me is to be clear about my priorities and to make sure that my time, energy, and passion align with them in the right order. I enjoy writing, but honestly, I couldn't care less about it compared to my love for my wife and kids. And although I greatly appreciate the academy, I'm first and foremost a local-church guy.

"The second challenge for me is choosing what to focus my studies on. So many options, so little time. Do I write something scholarly or popular? Do I keep working on my specialization, or do I branch out to something new? To succeed in this area requires a sober understanding of my own limits and a good dose of God's wisdom."

What Are a Few Practical Steps You Have Found Helpful in Realizing the Vision of the Ecclesial Theologian?

"First, perhaps the greatest joy and catalyst for my calling is community. Once a month, I meet with a group of guys in South Central LA to read each other's work and encourage one another in writing. I've also started organizing an annual atonement symposium of scholars who are researching or writing on the doctrine of atonement. These are structures that I've built into my life that challenge me intellectually and encourage me to press forward in writing.

"Second, finding areas of overlap has been my most effective strategy in maintaining scholarly and ecclesial pursuits. When I needed to write a document for my church on divorce and remarriage, I used my research to also write an article that is being published separately. When our church hosted an event at Pauley Pavilion (UCLA) about theology and sports, I read loads of scholarship on the topic, gave an accessible talk to an audience full of athletes and coaches, and now I'll be presenting on the topic at an academic conference and hopefully writing more.

"Third, maintaining a disciplined schedule is essential. This plays out in two ways. As a pastor, I set aside two whole days every week for study (including reading, sermon prep, and writing); all of which are geared toward church-related tasks. At home (that is, outside of my church hours), my goal is to write for one hour a day. Ideally, this happens early in the morning, sometimes it's at night after everyone else is asleep. A little time every day makes a great difference in the long-term vision of being a pastor theologian."

Strategy Six: Refer to the Place Where You Work as "Your Study"

Never, under pain of excommunication from the ecclesial-theologian club, refer to your study as an "office." If this is the first time you've heard this rule, you get three free passes to break the habit. After that, your ecclesial-theologian license will be suspended!

The fact is, semantics matter, and nomenclature counts. If you call your study an office, people in your church will have a certain set of expectations regarding what you do during the day. Offices are where people make phone calls and type emails and have meetings. But if you refer to the place where you work as your study, your congregants will come to have a different set of expectations—more in line with the sort of work done by an ecclesial theologian. The room with your books, where you study the Scriptures and pray and write—that room is your study. Start referring to it as such, and your congregation will come to see studying as central to your calling.

Practically speaking, you may find it helpful to work in two different locations. Of course, this isn't a luxury everyone can afford. But we've found it useful to have one space in which to study and another for more administrative duties. Todd generally studies in an attic study at home, and Gerald in a basement study at the church. (No doubt, our choice of locations reveals something subtle about our personalities; what that is, we're not yet sure). It is important to have our primary study space away from the traffic, making it easier to focus on work. Even so, we still refer to each location as a study, because, you'll remember, ecclesial theologians don't have offices — they have studies, sometimes even two!

Strategy Seven: Build Study-and-Writing Leave into Your Schedule

At our church, each full-time ministry staff person gets one study week a year and is encouraged to take it. A dedicated week, focused exclusively on a reading or writing project, allows one to make more gains in one week than is possible in four or five one-day units. The continuity of thought and the space to brood without distraction are precious commodities. Typically, most pastors have a bit of a downtime in the calendar year when things aren't quite as busy. Schedule your study time around such times.

If you manage your own schedule, then you have no excuses. For those who aren't in control of their calendar, or who can't write into their contract an extra week of study, we encourage you to make a case to your board or supervisor. Draft a short letter requesting the writing leave, and explain how such leave will benefit your ministry and your personal health.

Along the same lines, begin making noise early on about a sabbatical. Many churches will embrace a sabbatical policy, especially if you ask far enough in advance. At our church, we have a sabbatical policy that gives three months after seven years of service. Sabbaticals should be carefully thought through, and the aims and goals should be clearly spelled out ahead of time for both the pastor and the church. And if done right, this is a great way to accomplish a significant research project. Just as a study week is more effective than five independent study days, so too a sabbatical allows the ecclesial theologian more significant space to focus than what can be achieved in smaller blocks of time. And beyond the extended length of time, a sabbatical has the advantage of allowing you to change locations—perhaps settle into a university or college context where you can have more direct access to theological resources.

Strategy Eight: Recruit a Pastor-Theologian Intern

Many churches have internship programs for all sorts of ministry areas—youth, children, music, discipleship, outreach. We suggest that ecclesial theologians follow this same pattern, yet they should also focus an internship on the duties of an ecclesial theologian. We happen to have the good fortune of being near a number of theology schools. Because of this, we have a fair number of students who attend our church, many of whom resonate with our vision for the ecclesial theologian. Two of these graduate students currently serve as "pastor-theologian" interns, and we work hard to give them exposure to all aspects of the ecclesial-theologian vision. This means engaging them in the customary conversations on leadership, preaching, and pastoral care. But it also means that we engage them in our respective research projects. They are eager to help, have much to contribute, and function in a comparable way to that of a research assistant to a university or divinity school professor.

This partnership has been enormously fruitful for both parties. It has allowed us to expand our research in directions we otherwise would not have had time to do, and it has given these young men a firsthand look at the day-to-day work of an ecclesial theologian. So keep an eye out for motivated graduate students who resonate with your calling and vision for pastoral ministry. They will welcome the opportunity to learn from your example and engage with you in your research and writing projects, and you will reap the benefits of their involvement.

Case Study: John Yates

Dr. John Yates serves as rector (senior pastor) of Holy Trinity Anglican Church in Raleigh, North Carolina, a ten-year-old church plant. Holy Trinity is a middle/upper-middle-class church of about five hundred active adults and children that draws from a broad geographic region. For the past ten years, the church has worshiped in a prep school chapel, and is currently building a church facility four blocks from the state capitol in the heart of downtown Raleigh. John completed his PhD in New Testament at Cambridge in 2006, where he examined the role of the Spirit in creation and new creation in the letters of Paul. While doing his research, he served part-time as a chaplain at one of the Cambridge colleges.

He answers our questions as follows.

What Are Your Greatest Challenges as You Seek to Embody the Ecclesial-Theologian Vision?

"Of course the single greatest challenge is time. There is not enough! This will always be the most significant constraint on the work of an ecclesial theologian. It means I need to be highly efficient in the ways I use my time. It means I have to learn to be content with producing less work more slowly. And it means I have to resist the temptation to rush."

What Are a Few Practical Steps You Have Found Helpful in Realizing the Vision of the Ecclesial Theologian?

"The first thing an aspiring ecclesial theologian must do is gain perspective on the nature of our work. If time is our single greatest constraint, it is also the ecclesial theologian's secret weapon. Academic theologians live under intense pressure to publish or perish. Their careers hang in the balance as deadlines loom. The ecclesial theologian should feel no such pressure. In fact, the work we want to produce will of necessity take more time than academic research. We should give it time and tend it carefully.

"I once had dinner with Professor Colin Gunton shortly after a conference presentation by a theologian in her late thirties. I asked what he thought of the paper, and after a pause, he replied that he thought it was good but that he did not expect much of younger theologians. He went on to explain that it takes decades to produce good theology and that he tends to withhold judgment on a person's work until much later in his or her career. As a would-be theologian in my late twenties at the time, I found his words both refreshing and challenging. The pressure to produce a great work before I turned thirty was lifted, but the gauntlet had been thrown down. In order to produce one good work before turning fifty, I was going to have to labor diligently, producing second-rate material for several decades! Be patient. Take the long road.

"On a more practical level, the most important thing that I do each year is to block out several study days per quarter. During this time (forty-eight to seventy-two hours) I go away by myself and stay at a friend's vacation home. I take a box of books with me and try to focus my work on one main project and one smaller project, giving myself the freedom to jump back and forth between the two. I work about twelve hours each day and try my best not to touch email or return any phone calls. This focused time away is absolutely essential for maintaining momentum on projects and getting good work done."

Strategy Nine: Earn Buy-In from Your Church Leadership

Perhaps the chief concern of aspiring ecclesial theologians is whether their church leadership will support this particular aspect of their pastoral calling. Or will they, as many fear, look askance at their research and writing, concluding that it is at best extracurricular, if not distracting. This is a valid concern and one we've heard articulated many times by both frustrated ecclesial theologians and concerned laity alike. While most church boards will recognize the value of serious study, especially that which is geared toward preaching and teaching, some will want to question whether theological scholarship is really the best use of their already busy pastor's time. If you find yourself in such a context, you will need to proceed slowly.

We need to remember that because theology has been divorced from the church for so long it is no longer obvious to many congregations that sustained theological engagement is a good thing for pastors. This is where you may need to do a little teaching and point out how the church has suffered from this parting of the ways. You will also want to gently point out that just like teaching a book of the Bible forces you to understand it at a deeper level, even more so, putting your thoughts on paper helps you achieve levels of clarity that would otherwise not be possible. In a similar vein, it is important for your church's leadership to come to terms with your unique gifting and wiring, and to begin to embrace the fact that by granting you time to engage in theological scholarship, you are refreshed and invigorated for your other pastoral duties. Furthermore, you can cast vision for the fact that your church has a responsibility not only to its own local fellowship, but to the larger *ecclesia* of God, insofar as God in his grace would allow you to have such a ministry.

These are just some suggestions we've found useful in our context. But the bottom line is this: Your church will need to *see* the value of theological scholarship to your ministry, *not* simply hear you *argue* for it. This means you must begin by being a good pastor who loves your flock and desires to see the gospel flourish in their lives. As you do that faithfully, your church's leadership will, over time, come to trust you and how you spend your time; they'll see that you're committed to putting first things first. And while they may never fully get why you like to write journal articles or read hefty tomes no one has ever heard of, if they are well-loved and cared for, they will probably be happy to let you manage your time as you think best.

Strategy Ten: Let the Necessity of Love Trump Your Love of Truth

Finally, and most importantly, remember that your primary responsibility as an ecclesial theologian is to be a theologian to your own church. No one wants to be used, especially not your church. That precious blood-bought gift of God's grace is not a platform for you to indulge your fancy for scholarship, nor a venue for you to cloister yourself off from the nitty-gritty of your calling. In fact, if your congregation starts to begrudge your study time (for example, if you hear things like "He spends all his time holed up in his office"), you will need to take a close look at your priorities. It may be that your congregation is serving a vital role in your own sanctification by calling into question the degree to which your study time is really in the service of Christ and his kingdom.

As a pastor, you should consider everything in light of the needs of your church. We have referred to Augustine before, and he proves a useful example at this point too. Even though Augustine was a brilliant theologian who bequeathed to the church a rich legacy of writings, he was chiefly motivated by the on-the-ground needs of his congregation. Augustine let the necessity of love trump his love of truth. "Augustine's desire for knowledge was tempered by his duty to love his neighbor. Those things that did not make ample use of his time and did not exhibit love towards others were deemed as less important."[14] Following Augustine's example does not mean everything you do will have a direct or an immediate impact on your congregation. But your flock must know that they are your top priority, central in the orbit of your affections, even before Barth or Bonhoeffer or the *Bulletin of Biblical Research*.

---

14. See Anthony C. Thornhill, "Scholarship and Ministry in the Life and Thought of Augustine" *Eleutheria* 1:2 (2011): 107–14 (cf. 111–12).

Theology serves the church, not the other way around; she's a hand-maiden, not a god. If in a pastor's quest to serve the church universal he neglects the church local, those to whom he has a very concrete commitment, then one ought to wonder if he is really serving the church at all. Besides, all our scholarship ought to drive us deeper into our love for God and his people. If it's not, then what are we really studying for?

CHAPTER 9

The Future of a Movement, the Renewal of the Church

I have not run away from being your shepherd.[1]

The Prophet Jeremiah

Throughout this book, we have argued that the renewal of the church depends on a renewal of the church's theology. We have likewise argued that this theological renewal depends on the resurrection of the ancient vision of the pastor as ecclesial theologian. It is the pastoral community, we've been at pains to show, that bears the primary responsibility for the theological integrity of God's people. Churches won't rise above the theological level of their leaders; as go the shepherds, so go the sheep.

Of course, not every pastor will be an ecclesial theologian, just as not every pastor will be an exceptional preacher or leader or counselor. Pastors have different gifts. But for the sake of the church, it is high time to hold out the historic ideal of the pastor as ecclesial theologian.

In previous chapters, we've alluded to the sort of institutional changes necessary for seeing this vision realized. It simply will not happen without intentional effort on the part of a whole host of people, especially pastors, professors, and students. And so, in drawing this book to a close, we would like to offer three parting words to these three constituencies, followed by a concluding prayer, since we truly believe that the vision of this book will only come to pass through the divine miracle of resurrection!

A Word to Professors: Play the Part of John the Baptist

Although many have sought to bridge the gap between the world of theology and the world of the church, they have found limited success. We believe this is because such efforts continue to assume, and then work

---

1. Jeremiah 17:16.

within, the present division of labor between the academy and the church. Both academic theologians and pastors work with the assumption that those with exceptional intellectual gifting ought to pursue a career in the academy, while those with pastoral gifting ought to pursue a calling in the church. This assumption must be dragged into the street and bludgeoned to death. And we are asking that you, as a professor, help wield the blunt instrument.

We have no grievance with bright Christians pursuing careers in the academy; in fact, may your tribe increase! But the parting of the ways between the academy and the church has so reshaped the pastoral vocation that the latter has lost its rightful theological identity. And as we've come to see, theologically passive pastors only perpetuate the perception that theological acumen is largely an "academic" concern. But this only further exacerbates the problem. Now the intellectually gifted gravitate toward the academy as the only option for theological leadership, further draining the theological integrity of the church. And on the cycle goes, to the detriment of both the church and theology.

If we're to see a resurgence of theological integrity in our churches, we will need to promote pastoral ministry as a viable context for theological leadership. We will need to envision a future in which those with both intellectual gifting and a pastoral heart can use those gifts to the fullest extent possible in the church. This is not to say that every pastor must be a published theologian. But it is to say that the pastoral community must reimagine its vocation to include taking primary responsibility for the theological leadership of the church.

Now, as an academic theologian, you play a vital role in reimagining the pastoral vocation. You are in a position of significant influence, whether you realize it or not. The fact is, you are perceived by the emerging generation of pastors and theologians as a theological leader of the church. Because of this, the cues you send to the next generation carry tremendous weight. What signals are your students picking up from you as they look to you for guidance about their calling? What possibilities do you help them imagine? And are you willing to play the role of John the Baptist by directing many of your disciples, perhaps your best and brightest, away from your own vocation to the pastoral ministry? He must increase; I must decrease.

At least some of your students are torn between the life of the mind and the life of the church. They enjoy studying, love writing, and get juiced on scholarship. They resonate deeply with your sense of vocation and have the desire and gifting to serve as thought-leaders to the broader evangelical community. But they also have a heart for the church and for pastoral ministry. They enjoy people, love preaching, and are energized by leadership. And if their experience is like ours, they find themselves at a vocational fork in the road, which can trigger an identity crisis. Will they subdue their intellectual aspirations for a career in the church or lay aside their pastoral desires for a career in the academy?

For those who find themselves at this juncture, your affirmation of the vision of the ecclesial theologian is vital. If you would be willing to validate the possibilities of a theological vocation *within* the church, they would be far more likely to embrace it. A word of encouragement from you will no doubt go a long way. During our student days, a number of professors cast a vision for the importance of a theologically robust pastoral ministry, and their advocacy was instrumental in our discerning our calling and shaping our identity as pastor theologians.

So please do not underestimate the role you play in directing the next generation of pastors and theologians. If you perpetuate the present division of labor between the academy and the church, your students will likely follow suit. But if you hold out the vision of the ecclesial theologian as a viable alternative, some of your students may find their way into a future that utilizes the full range of their gifts and desires.

A Word to Pastors: Embrace the Gap

Pastors often lament the gap between the academy and the church, or the doing of theology and the practice of ministry. Yet these laments belie the fact that we have made peace with the present division of labor. We delegate to the academy the task of providing theological leadership to the church, then complain about what we in turn get from the academy. But could the problem be less with the academy and more with the church, which has outsourced its responsibility to the academy?

There was a day when there was no gap between the academy and the church precisely because there was no academy. And when the academy emerged in the twelfth century, it functioned as a formal extension of the church's mission. But with the dawn of the Enlightenment, the university context shifted toward an overtly secular posture and at the same time gradually came to replace the church as *the* established and recognized institution of intellectual learning. Given the university's dominating influence, it was absolutely vital that Nicene Christianity maintain a vibrant voice within its walls, and we pastors should be grateful that Christian intellectuals moved—and have remained—in this context. But given the new academic social location for Christian theologians, it has been a mistake for us to ask those same intellectuals to continue servicing the theological needs of the church *in the same way*.

The academy represents its own legitimate realm of discourse, and we should be grateful it exists. It has led to advances in all kinds of learning, and it is vital that we have Christian intellectuals and theologians and Bible scholars interacting directly with the other fields of discourse represented in the academy. The questions of the academy aren't going away, and we need Christian intellectuals present there to provide cogent Christian responses. But the pastoral community errs insofar as we think that theology done in the academy is going to have the same agenda and ecclesial dialect that it once did when it was being done by pastors in the churches. That's an unfair burden to place upon academic theologians. The problem between the academy and the church is not the "gap"; the gap is inevitable. The problem is that we are asking academic theologians to shoulder the burdens of two distinct social locations. We are asking the academy to do our job.

The pastoral community needs to free up our academic brethren to be *academic*. It's what they are best suited to do, and it's the best way they can make a unique and vital contribution to the church. But they cannot—from the social location of the academy—service *all* the theological needs of the church. Asking that academic theologians solve both academic problems and pastoral problems with equal acumen only creates inevitable frustration and misplaced expectations.

This is not to say that academic theologians have nothing to offer the church. But it is to say that the academy and the church represent two distinct fields of discourse, with their own unique concerns, agendas, questions, and audiences. The sooner we raise up a new generation of pastor theologians to address such questions, the sooner both the academy and the church can get on with what they are good at.

If you are a pastor with strong intellectual and theological gifting, then we charge you—in the sight of God and the elect angels!—that you not bury this talent in the ground. Questions regarding anthropology, atonement, epistemology, eschatology, etc., are too important to outsource to the academy. The church needs pastors who are capable of connecting—with robust intellectual integrity—the deep truths of God and our contemporary context. We need pastors who are able to assess the underlying assumptions of our culture and who are able to offer, on behalf of the larger church, cogent responses to that culture. We need pastors conversant in the biblical languages who are able to mine the Word of God for the health of God's people. We need pastors who read Irenaeus and Augustine, Hegel and Kant, and who have the intellectual gifting and vocational capacity to offer distinctly pastoral appropriations of such seminal thinkers.

Do not neglect the gift that has been given you or fall prey to the mistaken assumption that academic theologians are sufficient for meeting all the theological needs of the church. We appeal to you to help create a future in which the pastoral community no longer adopts a largely passive role with respect to theological leadership.

A Word to Students: Believe!

The present bifurcation between theology and the church will not be overcome in a single generation. The trenches have been dug too deeply, the road forked too sharply. Yet the bifurcation can be overcome. The future of the ecclesial-theologian movement and the renewal of the church rest with the students who will emerge in the next decades as the theological and pastoral leaders of the church. If you, as did we, find yourself pulled between two seemingly diverging vocations, rest assured that not only can these two vocations be brought together into a single vocation, but know that embracing this single vocation is vital to the health and integrity of God's people.

Not all of you are called to the ecclesial-theologian vision. Some of you will be called to other aspects of pastoral ministry. And some of you will be directed by the Lord into an academic context. But many of you are being called by the Lord to bring the full weight of your intellectual and pastoral gifting into the church. Do not neglect this calling, nor dismiss it as a diminutive use of your theological gifting. It is a difficult vision to live out, to be sure. But it is possible.

We offer here a small sampling of the work being done by the pastors of the Center for Pastor Theologians as evidence that such a project is indeed feasible:

- Rev. Matthew Mason, an Anglican pastor in Salisbury, is looking to Irenaeus's concept of human maturation as a framework for constructing a response to contemporary anthropology and sexuality.
- Dr. Ryan Jackson, a Pentecostal pastor in North Carolina, is working on a project that seeks to construct a healthy relationship between experience and Scripture.
- Dr. John Yates, an Anglican pastor in North Carolina, is editing a seven-volume series on Anglican catechesis.
- Dr. David Rudolph, a Messianic rabbi in Virginia, continues to publish important scholarly and theological work on the contemporary relationship between the Jewish and Christian communities.
- Dr. Greg Thompson, a Presbyterian pastor in Virginia, is exploring the pastoral and theological implications of the work of James Davidson Hunter.

More examples from the Center could be listed, but the salient point has been made; it is possible to be an ecclesial theologian.

The church stands in great need of pastors who are capable of functioning as robust theologians, for the sake of the church and its theology. It is our hope and prayer that those of you now preparing to serve the church will take seriously the need for, and believe in the possibility of, the ecclesial theologian. And it is our prayer that those gifted for such a vision would answer the call as our Lord directs.

Conclusion: A Prayer

Oh God, grant it that your church may flourish. Grant it that your people would come more fully to believe—to truly believe—that Christ is risen, that he has ascended, that he sits at your right hand, and that he comes again to judge the living and the dead. May we, your people, be found ready for his return and busy doing his work.

And may those of us who carry pastoral responsibility discharge our duties with integrity, authenticity, and skill. Grant it that we would follow the example of the Great Shepherd—our own Shepherd and Lord, laying down our lives for our sheep and serving your people in humility and love. Let us not neglect the gifts that you have given us, gifts that have not been given to us for our own sake alone, but for the sake of your people whom you have called us to serve. May their good and your glory be the highest aim of our hearts, and in this way, may we fulfill the two greatest commandments.

And Father, we ask that he who ascended on high would once again give gifts to the church. We ask that through his grace you would raise up a new generation of pastors who are uniquely capable of intellectually navigating the rich textures of your world. Give us pastors who have the wisdom and insight to lead us through the dark valley of sin and death and suffering into the glorious light of truth; you are that truth. Through them, may you teach us to believe, and in believing, love.

In the name of your Son, Jesus Christ, we pray. Amen.

Acknowledgments

Writing a book costs something, and it is often the families of the authors who pay the bill. So it was here. We are grateful to our wives and children, who bore patiently with our already too busy schedules.

We are thankful to Peter Leithart, Doug Sweeney, Kevin Hector, Mickey Klink, and Matthew Mason for reading and commenting on early drafts of the manuscript. Their input helped to strengthen the book at key points.

Ryan Pazdur, our editor at Zondervan, has been a pleasure to work with, and we are grateful for his careful and thoughtful interaction with the project.

Max Clayton, Zach Wagner, and Nathan Suire—three of the sharpest students we know—deserve special recognition for their labors in helping cull through the hundreds of bibliographies represented in Migne's *Patrologia Graeca, Patrologia Latina,* and the two Alexander Street Press collections (see the appendix). This was no mean feat and added a layer of "flesh and bone" to our historical survey in chapter 2 that would have been difficult to achieve otherwise.

Our church family at Calvary Memorial Church in Oak Park deserves our gratitude—and indeed has it! Our congregation has generously and graciously released us to work on theological projects that benefit the wider church (of which this book is one), and we count ourselves blessed to serve such a wonderful body of believers.

And, most especially, we wish to acknowledge our sincere affection to the Fellows of the Center for Pastor Theologians—to whom this book is dedicated—for their feedback, friendship, and encouragement over the past eight years. These fellow sojourners have been living examples of pastor theologians, and their real-time experience has shaped this project, and our lives, in many intangible ways.

A Survey of the Ratio of Clerical, Nonclerical, and Monastic Theologians

Contained within *Patrologia Graeca*, *Patrologia Latina*,
The Digital Library of Classic Protestant Texts, and
The Digital Library of the Catholic Reformation

To help orient ourselves to the larger narrative of the pastor theologian, we analyzed the vocational context of the authors found in four major collections: Jacques-Paul Migne's *Patrologia Graeca*; Migne's *Patrologia Latina*; the Alexander Street Press's *The Digital Library of Classic Protestant Texts,* and its twin, *The Digital Library of the Catholic Reformation*. The four collections are uniquely insightful, given the breadth of their scope. Collectively, they include over five hundred authors and span nearly the whole of the first eighteen centuries of the church.

Jacques-Paul Migne's two collections constitute a massive nineteenth-century compilation of theological texts from the fathers and doctors of the church as well as other Christian writers. Together, the two compilations consist of nearly four hundred print volumes (217 in the Latin series, 161 in the Greek series) and represent the largest collection of ancient extant texts in print. Collectively, Migne's two compilations span the history of the church from the days of the Apostolic Fathers to the fifteenth century. (The Latin series ends in 1200, while the Greek series carries a handful of authors into the fifteenth century.) The two series, published from 1841–66, are no longer in print, though a few research libraries (Yale, Harvard, Penn State) have put their collections online via scanned copies.[1]

Subsequent gains in textual criticism and historical scholarship have resulted in more accurate texts for many of the Latin and Greek authors found in Migne's collections (see, for example, the collection *Sources*

---

1. See classicsindex.wikispaces.com/migne_PG for the Greek collection, and classicsindex. wikispaces.com/migne_PL for the Latin collection.

Chrétiennes, founded in 1942 in Lyon by the Jesuits Jean Daniélou, Claude Mondésert, and Henri de Lubac). However, Migne's collections are the most accessible and comprehensive, and they remain the standard for citation and reference. Insofar as our aim was not an examination of the texts themselves, but rather establishing a canon of Christian writers, Migne's collections were the best choice for exploring the first twelve centuries of church history.

The two Alexander Street Press collections do for the sixteenth and seventeenth centuries what Migne did for the first fifteen. These collections pull together the writings of Protestant and Catholic authors following the turmoil of the Protestant Reformation and Catholic Counter-Reformation up until the dawn of the Enlightenment. As with Migne, these collections are meant to be comprehensive for the period they cover. *The Digital Library of Classic Protestant Texts* contains the writings of two hundred authors, and *The Digital Library of the Catholic Reformation* contains one hundred and forty.[2]

Throughout our survey, we have assigned each author in these collections one of three labels: *clerical* (e.g., bishop, priest), *nonclerical* (e.g., university professor, independent scholar), or *monastic*.[3] Our main objective in analyzing these collections was to see concrete examples of how the church has historically made space for parish clergy to function as scholars and theologians. Thus, we have classified a theologian as clerical only if he actually oversaw a parish or diocese, or was otherwise formally involved in church administration (e.g., as a cardinal) for a significant segment of his career.

Our definition of cleric is, of course, fairly narrow given the historically pervasive role of the church in the larger society—especially from the Middle Ages up until the Enlightenment. This is particularly true in the twelfth century and beyond, after the advent of the universities. The worlds of the university (where teachers of theology were required to take holy orders), the regular clergy (who lived according to a "rule" within a cloistered community), the secular clergy (who served out in the world as parish priests), the mendicant monks (who ministered out in the world,

2. Both Alexander Street collections are fully searchable web-based archives. For detailed information on these collections, see http://alexanderstreet.com/products/digital-library-catholic-reformation and http://alexanderstreet.com/products/digital-library-classic-protestant-texts.

3. Here, we must acknowledge the help of three exceptional graduate students: Max Clayton, Zach Wagner, and Nathan Suire, for their tireless labors in helping us sort through the requisite bibliographies. Any mistakes, however, remain our own.

but not in a particular parish), and regular monks (who lived in cloistered communities), all ran together in ways that do not make for easy distinctions between clerical, nonclerical, and monastic theologians.

Arguably, nearly all theologians between the thirteenth century up until the Enlightenment could be classified as clerical in one sense or another. But insofar as our primary aim in this book is to reconnect parish ministry with theological scholarship, we have chosen to limit our definition of cleric. Thus, though Thomas Aquinas was ordained a Dominican priest, his career was that of university professor; consequently, he is identified in our survey as a nonclerical theologian. In the case where scholars transitioned between clerical and nonclerical vocations (as was frequently the case during and after the Reformation), we have classified them based on the primary vocation of their career. For instance, though Peter Lombard spent the final year of his life as the Bishop of Paris, the bulk of his career was nonclerical, and we have classified him as such in our survey.

An executive summary of all four collections is offered in the table below. Notably, clerical theologians are numerically dominant (even if only slightly) in three of the four collections.

Collection	Clerical	Nonclerical	Monastic
Migne Greek Fathers (90–1500)	46	31	15
Migne Latin Fathers (90–1200)	67	22	40
Library of Classic Protestant Texts (1500–1750)	102	98	0
Library of the Catholic Reformation (1500–1750)	42	71	27
Total	257	222	82

Summary by Time Period for All Collections

Our survey in chapter 2 is divided into five main time periods, each of which represents a distinct shift in the vocational context of the theologian: Apostolic Fathers to Constantine (90–300), Constantine to the monasteries (300–600), monasteries to the universities (600–1200), universities to the Reformation (1200–1500), and the Reformation to the Enlightenment (1500–1750). Our analysis of the Migne and Alexander Street Press collections follows the same division.

Assessed in broad terms, the ratios in Migne and Alexander Street Press reflect the same basic contours as our survey in chapter two. In Migne, clerical theologians are numerically dominant up until 1200, which represents the advent of the universities. Following the universities, especially in the Protestant Tradition, clerical and nonclerical theologians both have a significant—nearly equal—presence in the Alexander Street Press collections.

The graph below offers an executive summary of the ratio of clerical, nonclerical, and monastic theologians for all four collections, broken down according to our five periods. (Note: Migne's collection includes a very small sampling for 1200–1500—only fifteen Greek authors. As such, the picture it offers us during this time is quite sketchy. We have included it here, however, for the sake of completeness.) Following the summary graph are the data for each of the four collections.

Ratio of Clerical, Nonclerical, and Monastic Theologians in Migne (90–1500) and Alexander Street Press (1500–1750)

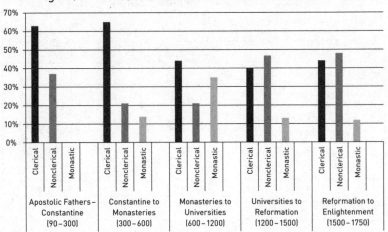

Migne's *Patrologia Graeca*

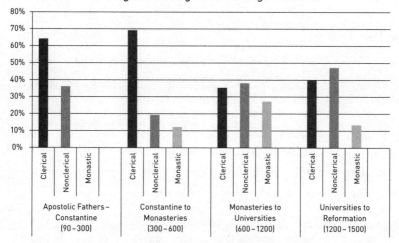

Ratio of Clerical, Nonclerical, and Monastic Theologians in Migne's *Patrologia Graeca*

Classification of Authors in Migne's *Patrologia Graeca*, by Time Period

Apostolic Fathers to Constantine (90–300)			
Clement of Rome	1st century	Clerical	Bishop of Rome
Ignatius of Antioch	c. 35–107	Clerical	Third Bishop of Antioch
Polycarp	69–155	Clerical	2nd-century Christian Bishop of Smyrna
Justin Martyr	c. 100–165	Nonclerical	Philosopher, Christian apologist
Irenaeus	c. 130–200	Clerical	Bishop of Lyon
Clement of Alexandria	c. 150–215.	Nonclerical	Head of the catechetical school of Alexandria
Gregory Thaumaturgus	c. 213–275	Clerical	Bishop
Hippolytus	c. 170–236	Clerical	Martyr, presbyter, Antipope of Rome

Apostolic Fathers to Constantine (90–300) continued			
(Sextus) Julius Africanus	c. 180–250	Nonclerical	Christian writer, traveler, and historian
Dionysius of Alexandria	c. 200–265	Clerical	Bishop of Alexandria, Egypt
Pamphilus of Caesarea	c. 240–310	Nonclerical	Head of Catechetical School
Origen	c. 185–254	Nonclerical	Ordained priest, but primarily a philosopher
Methodius of Olympus	c. ?–311	Clerical	Bishop of Olympus, then Bishop of Tyre
Eustathius of Antioch	c. 270–337	Clerical	Bishop of Beroea, then patriarch of Antioch
		C-9, NC-5, M-0	

Constantine to Monasteries (300–600)			
Titus of Bostra	c. 362–371	Clerical	Bishop
Eusebius of Caesarea	c. 260–340	Clerical	Bishop of Caesarea, church historian
Athanasius	c. 296–373	Clerical	Bishop of Alexandria and theologian
Basil of Caesarea	c. 329–379	Clerical	Bishop of Caesarea and theologian
Cyril of Jerusalem	c. 315–386	Clerical	Bishop of Jerusalem and theologian
Diodore of Tarsus	d. 390	Clerical	Bishop of Tarsus, head of monastery
Macarius (the great) of Egypt	c. 300–391	Monastic	Desert monk and hermit
Eusebius of Emesa	c. 300–360	Clerical	Bishop of Emesa
Macarius Alexandrinus	d. 394	Monastic	Nitrian monk
Gregory of Nazianzus	c. 330–389	Clerical	Archbishop of Constantinople

Constantine to Monasteries (300 – 600) continued			
Didymus (the Blind)	c. 313 – 398	Nonclerical	Head of the catechetical school of Alexandria
Epiphanius of Salamis	c. 310 – 403	Clerical	Bishop of Salamis, Cyprus
Gregory of Nyssa	c. 335 – 395	Clerical	Bishop of Nyssa
John Chrysostom	c. 347 – 407	Clerical	Archbishop of Constantinople
Proclus (the successor)	c. 412 – 485	Nonclerical	Philosopher
Severian of Gabala	4th century	Clerical	Bishop of Gabala
Philostorgius	c. 368 – 433	Nonclerical	Church historian
Synesius of Cyrene	c. 373 – 414	Clerical	Bishop of Ptolemais
Theodore of Mopsuestia	c. 350 – 428	Clerical	Bishop of Mopsuestia
Socrates of Constantinople	c. 380 – 450	Nonclerical	Church historian
Sozomen	c. 380 – 448	Nonclerical	Church historian
Cyril of Alexandria	c. 375 – 444	Clerical	Patriarch of Alexandria
Isidore of Seville	c. 570 – 636	Clerical	Archbishop of Seville
Nilus of Sinai	c. ? – 430	Monastic	Monk and abbot
Theodoret of Cyrus	c. 393 – 460	Clerical	Bishop of Cyrrhus, Syria
Basil of Seleucia	c. ? – 468	Clerical	Archbishop of Seleucia in Isauria
		C-18, NC-5, M-3	

Monasteries to Universities (600–1200)			
Leontius	c. 385–495	Clerical	Bishop of Fréjus
Leontius of Byzantium	c. 485–543	Monastic	Byzantine monk and theologian
Procopius of Gaza	4th–5th century	Nonclerical	Christian sophist and rhetorician
Sophronius of Jerusalem	c. 560–638	Clerical	Patriarch of Jerusalem
John Moschus	c. 540–619	Monastic	Byzantine monk and writer
Anastasius of Sinai	7th century	Monastic	Monk at Monastery of St. Catherine on Sinai
Maximus Confessor	c. 580–662	Monastic	Monk, abbot, and theologian
Hesychius of Jerusalem	c. ?–450	Clerical	Presbyter of Jerusalem
Leontius Neapoleos in Cypro	7th century	Clerical	Bishop of Neapolis
Johannes Damascenus	c. 675–749	Monastic	Monk
John Malalas	6th century	Nonclerical	Civil servant
Gregorius Agrigentinus	6th century	Clerical	Bishop of Agrigentum
Theodore the Studite	c. 759–826	Monastic	Monk and abbot
Nicephorus	c. 758–829	Clerical	Patriarch of Constantinople
Photius of Constantinople	c. 815–897	Clerical	Patriarch of Constantinople
Nicetas David Paphlagon	Late 9th century	Clerical	Bishop of Paphlagonia
Leo VI	c. 866–912	Nonclerical	Byzantine emperor
Theophanes	8th–9th century	Monastic	Monk and chronicler
George Hamartolos	9th century	Monastic	Monk

Monasteries to Universities (600–1200) continued			
Constantine Porphyrogenitus	c. 905–959	Nonclerical	Macedonian Emperor in Byzantine Empire
Symeon the Metaphrast	10th century	Nonclerical	Chronicler, honored as a saint
Leo Diaconus	10th century	Nonclerical	Byzantine historian and chronicler
Oecumenius	10th century	Clerical	Bishop of Trikka
John Xiphilinus	11th century	Monastic	Monk and preacher
Georgius Cedrenus	11th century	Nonclerical	Byzantine historian
Michael Psellos	11th century	Nonclerical	Byzantine, philosopher, politician, and historian
Theophylactus	c. 1050–1126	Clerical	Archbishop of Ohrid
Nicephorus Bryennius	11th century	Nonclerical	Byzantine general, statesman, and historian
Euthymius Zygabenus	12th century	Monastic	Monk and biblical commentator
Anna Comnena	c. 1083–1148	Nonclerical	Byzantine historian
Theophanes Cerameus	12th century	Clerical	Archbishop of Rossano in Calabria
Joannes Cinnamus	12th century	Nonclerical	Byzantine historian
Theodore Prodromos	12th century	Nonclerical	Byzantine writer
Joannes Zonaras	12th century	Nonclerical	Byzantine chronicler and theologian
Eustathius of Thessalonica	c. 1110–1198	Clerical	Archbishop and scholar
Theodore Balsamon	c. 1130–1195	Clerical	Patriarch of Antioch
Nicetas Choniates	c. 1155–1216	Nonclerical	Greek historian, theologian
		C-13, NC-14, M-10	

Universities to Reformation (1200 – 1500)			
John Beccus / Veccus	c. 1235 – 1297	Clerical	Patriarch of Constantinople
Nicephorus Blemmida	c. 1198 – 1272	Monastic	Monk and writer of Greek church
George Pachymeres	c. 1242 – 1310	Clerical	Byzantine Greek historian, philosopher
Nikephoros Kallistos Xanthopoulos	c. 1256 – 1335	Clerical	Greek church historian
Nicephorus Gregoras	c. 1295 – 1360	Nonclerical	Byzantine humanist scholar, philosopher
Gregory Palamas	c. 1296 – 1359	Clerical	Archbishop of Thessaloniki
Barlaam of Seminara	14th century	Nonclerical	Clergyman, humanist, a philologist
Manuel Calecas	died 1410	Monastic	Monk and theologian of the Byzantine Empire
John Cantacuzenus	c. 1292 – 1383	Nonclerical	Byzantine emperor then later became a monk
Manuel Palaeologus	c. 1350 – 1425	Nonclerical	Byzantine emperor
Georgius Codinus	14th century	Nonclerical	Author of Byzantine literature
Michael Glycas	12th century	Nonclerical	Byzantine historian, theologian, and mathematician
Laonicus Chalcondyles	1423 – 1490	Nonclerical	Byzantine Greek scholar, historian
Gennadius	c. 1400 – 1473	Clerical	Patriarch of Constantinople
Basilios Bessarion	15th century	Clerical	Cardinal, Byzantine humanist and theologian
		C-6, NC-7, M-2	

Migne's *Patrologia Latina*

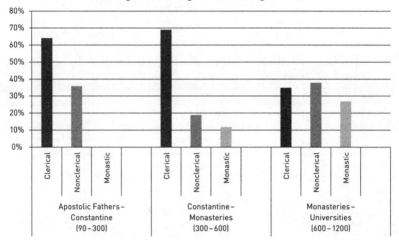

Ratio of Clerical, Nonclerical, and Monastic
Theologians in Migne's *Patrologia Latina*

Classification of Authors in Migne's *Patrologia Latina*, by Time Period

Apostolic Fathers to Constantine (90–300)			
Tertullian	c. 160–230	Unknown	Possibly lawyer; maybe priest later in life
Novatian	c. 200–c. 258	Clerical	The second antipope in papal history
Minucius Felix	c. 200–240	unknown	Apologist, doxographer
Cyprian	c. 200–258	Clerical	Bishop of Carthage
Arnobius	c. 3rd & 4th century	Nonclerical	Apologist, rhetoric teacher
Marcellinus	c. 3rd & 4th century	Clerical	Pope
Lactantius	c. 260–340	Nonclerical	Christian apologist, then Constantine's advisor
		C-3, NC-2, M-0	

Constantine to Monasteries (300–600)			
Constantine I "The Great"	c. 272–337	Nonclerical	Emperor of Rome
Hilary of Poitiers	c. 315–367	Clerical	Bishop of Poitiers
Zeno	c. 300–380	Clerical	Bishop of Verona
Optatus	c. 4th century	Clerical	Bishop of Milevis
Eusebius Vercellensis	c. 283–371	Clerical	Bishop in Italy
Firmicus Maternus, Julius	c. 4th century	Nonclerical	Probably from senatorial class
Filastrius (St. Philastrius)	c. 4th century	Clerical	Bishop of Brescia
Damasus 1st	c. 305–384	Clerical	Pope
Ambrose	c. 339–397	Clerical	Bishop of Milan
Ulfilas	c. 311–381	Clerical	Bishop, Bible translator, missionary to Goths
Caius Vettius Aquilinus Juvencus	c. 4th century	Clerical	Spanish poet and priest
Sulpicius Severus	c. 363–425	Monastic	Lawyer turned monk
Tyrannius Rufinus	c. 345–411	Monastic	Monk, theologian, historian, translator
Jerome	c. 342–420	Monastic	Various, monk, and Doctor of the Church
Orosius	c. 5th century	Clerical	Priest of Tarragona in Spain
Augustine	c. 354–430	Clerical	Bishop of Hippo
Marius Mercator	c. 390–451	Nonclerical	Latin writer
John Cassian	c. 360–435	Monastic	Monk, theologian
Prosper of Aquitaine	c. 390–463	Nonclerical	Various, layman who lived for a time with monks

Constantine to Monasteries (300–600) continued			
Petrus Chrysologus	c. 380–450	Clerical	Bishop of Ravenna
Salvian	5th century	Clerical	Priest on island of Lerins
Leo the Great	c. 400–461	Clerical	Pope
Maximus of Turin	c. 350–415	Clerical	Bishop of Turin
Sidonius Apollinarius	5th century	Clerical	Bishop of Clermont
Gelasius	c.?–496	Clerical	Pope
Prudentius	4th–5th century	Nonclerical	Poet and diplomat
Dracontius	c. 455–505	Nonclerical	Christian poet and lawyer
Paulinus of Nola	c. 354–431	Clerical	Bishop of Nola
Eugyppius	5th–6th century	Monastic	Monk, founded a monastery in Naples
Magnus Felix Ennodius	c. 474–521	Clerical	Bishop of Pavia
Boethius	c. 480–524	Nonclerical	Roman statesman, philosopher
Fulgentius	c. 480–550	Clerical	Bishop of Ruspe
		C-20, NC-7, M-5	

Monasteries to the Universities (600–1200)			
Benedict	c. 480–550	Monastic	Italian monk
Dionysius Exiguus	c. ?–556	Monastic	Scythian monk
Arator	6th century	Clerical	Subdeacon at Rome
Primasius	6th century	Clerical	Bishop of Hadrumetum
Cassiodorus	c. 485–580	Monastic	Monk at Vivarium

Monasteries to the Universities (600 – 1200) continued			
Gregory of Tours	c. 538 – 594	Clerical	Bishop of Tours
Gregory the Great	c. 540 – 604	Clerical	Pope
Isidore of Seville	c. 560 – 636	Clerical	Archbishop of Seville
Venantius Fortunatus	c. 530 – 610	Clerical	Bishop of Poitiers
Bede	c. 673 – 735	Monastic	Monk, historian, and theologian
Ildephonsus	c. 607 – 670	Clerical	Archbishop of Toledo
Leodegar	c. 616 – 678	Clerical	Bishop of Autun
Charlemagne	c. 742 – 814	Nonclerical	King of Franks, Roman emperor
Paulinus of Aquileia	c. 730 – 802	Clerical	Bishop of Aquileia
Alcuin	c. 735 – 804	Nonclerical	Invited by Charlemagne to be scholar and teacher
Smaragdus	c. 760 – 840	Monastic	Abbot of St. Mihiel and Castellio
Sedulius Scotus	9th century	Nonclerical	Grammarian, teacher, and Scripture commentator
Benedict of Aniane	c. 750 – 821	Monastic	Founder of monasteries
Agobard	c. 769 – 840	Clerical	Archbishop of Lyon
Theodulf	c. 750 – 821	Clerical	Bishop of Orleans
Gregory IV	c. 826 – 844	Clerical	Cardinal Priest of St. Marco, then later became Pope
Hrabanus Maurus	c. 780 – 856	Clerical	Archbishop of Mainz
Walafrid Strabo	c. 808 – 849	Monastic	Benedictine abbot

Monasteries to the Universities (600–1200) continued			
Leo IV	c. ?–855	Clerical	Pope
Haimo of Auxerre	c. 840–870	Monastic	Monk of St. Germanus
Nicholas I	c. 800–867	Clerical	Pope
Paschasius Radbertus	c. 790–865	Monastic	Abbot of Corbie
Ratramnus Corbeiensis	9th century	Monastic	Monk and Carolingian theologian
John Scotus Eriugena	c. 810–877	Nonclerical	Irish teacher, theologian, philosopher, and poet
Ado Viennensis	c. 800–875	Clerical	Monk, then Archbishop of Vienne
Usuard	c. 800–877	Monastic	Benedictine monk of St-Germain-des-Prés
Carolus Calvus "Charles the Bald"	c. 823–877	Nonclerical	Roman Emperor
Hincmarus Rhemensis	c. 806–882	Clerical	Archbishop of Reims
Anastasius Bibliothecarius	9th century	Nonclerical	Librarian and Greek scholar
Notker Balbulus	c. 840–912	Monastic	Benedictine monk, scholar, and poet
Odo Cluniacensis	c. 878–942	Monastic	Abbot of Cluny
Atto Vercellensis	9th–10th century	Clerical	Bishop of Vercelli
Flodoardus	c. 893–966	Clerical	A Canon of Reims
Ratherius	c. 887–974	Clerical	Bishop of Verona
Liutprand of Cremona	c. 920–972	Clerical	Bishop of Cremona
Hrotsvitha of Gandersheim	c. 935–973	Nonclerical	Female poet
Adso of Montier-en-der	c. 930–992	Monastic	Benedictine abbot and monk

Monasteries to the Universities (600–1200) continued			
Richerus S. Remigii	10th century	Monastic	Monk of Saint-Remi
Sylvester II	c. 940–1003	Clerical	Pope
Burchardus Vormatiensis	c. 965–1025	Clerical	Bishop of Worms
Fulbertus Carnotensis	c. 960–1028	Clerical	Bishop of Chartres
Bruno Herbipolensis	c. 1005–1045	Clerical	Bishop of Würzburg
Hermannus Contractus	c. 1013–1054	Nonclerical	Chronicler, mathematician, and poet
Petrus Damianus	c. 1007–1072	Clerical	Bishop Cardinal
Othlonus S. Emmerammi	c. 1010–1072	Monastic	German Benedictine monk and schoolmaster
Joannes Abrincensis	11th century	Clerical	Bishop of Avranches and then Archbishop of Rouen
Gregory VII	c. 1025–1085	Clerical	Monk then Pope
Victor III	c. 1026–1087	Monastic	Abbot, then briefly Pope
Lanfrancus Cantuariensis	c. 1010–1089	Clerical	Archbishop of Canterbury
Urbanus II	c. 1042–1099	Clerical	Monk, then Bishop, then Cardinal, then Pope
Hugo Flaviniacensis	11th century	Monastic	Benedictine monk and abbot
Godefridus Bullonius	c. 1060–1100	Nonclerical	Frankish knight
Guibertus S. Mariae de Novigento	c. 1053–1124	Monastic	Abbot of Nogent
Goffridus Vindocinensis	c. 1065–1132	Clerical	Abbot, then Cardinal
Anselm	c. 1033–1109	Clerical	Archbishop of Canterbury

Monasteries to the Universities (600 – 1200) continued			
Sigebertus Gemlacensis	c. 1030 – 1112	Monastic	Monk at Gembloux
Paschalis II	11th – 12th century	Clerical	Pope
Baldricus Dolensis	1050 – 1130	Clerical	Bishop of Dol en-Bretagne
Rupertus Tuitiensis	1075 – 1129	Monastic	Abbot of Deutz Abbey
Hildebertus Turonensis	c. 1056 – 1133	Clerical	Bishop of Le Mans
Honorius Augustodunensis	c. 1080 – c. 1150	Monastic	Monk near Ratisbon
Hugh of St. Victor	c. 1096 – 1142	Monastic	Canon regular of the monastery of St. Victor
Peter Abelard	c. 1079 – 1142	Monastic	Monk and teacher
William of Malmesbury	c. 1095 – 1143	Monastic	Librarian at Benedictine abbey
Eugenius III	c. ? – 1153	Clerical	Pope
Herveus	12th century	Monastic	Benedictine monk
Bernard of Clairvaux	c. 1090 – 1153	Monastic	Cistercian abbot
Odericus Vitalis	c. 1075 – 1142	Monastic	Benedictine monk
Peter the Venerable	c. 1092 – 1156	Monastic	Abbot of Cluny
Peter Lombard	c. 1100 – 1160	Nonclerical	Taught at Notre Dame, then briefly Bishop of Paris
Garnerius S. Victoris Walter	12th century	Monastic	Prior of St. Victor
Aelredus Rievallensis	c. 1110 – 1167	Monastic	Cistercian abbot
Richardus S. Victoris	c. ? – 1173	Monastic	Prior of St. Victor

Monasteries to the Universities (600–1200) continued			
Hildegard of Bingen	c. 1098–1179	Monastic	Abbess, mystic
John of Salisbury	c. 1115–1180	Clerical	Bishop of Chartres
Alexander III	c. 1105–1181	Clerical	Pope
William of Tyre	c. 1113–1186	Clerical	Archbishop of Tyre
Petrus Cellensis (Peter of Celle)	c. 1115–1183	Monastic	Benedictine abbot of Montier-la-Celle, briefly Bishop
Philippus de Harveng	12th century	Monastic	Abbot of Bonne-Esperance Abbey
Clement III	c. 1025–1100	Clerical	Antipope
Petrus Cantor	c. ?–1197	Nonclerical	Dean at Rheims
Celestine III	c. 1106–1198	Clerical	Pope
Martinus Legionensis	c. 1130–1203	Clerical	Priest and canon regular
Alanus de Insulis	c. ?–1203	Nonclerical	Teacher at Paris
Stephanus Tornacensis	c. 1130–1201	Clerical	Bishop of Tournai
Helinandus Frigidi Montis	c. 1160–1229	Nonclerical	Historical and didactic writer
Innocent III	c. 1160–1216	Clerical	Pope
		C-44, NC-13, M-35	

The Digital Library of Classic Protestant Texts

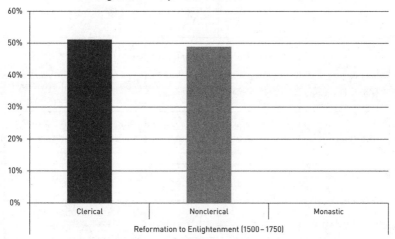

Ratio of Clerical, Nonclerical, and Monastic Theologians in
The Digital Library of Classic Protestant Texts

Reformation to Enlightenment (1500–1750)

Classification of Authors in
The Digital Library of Classic Protestant Texts

Reformation to Enlightenment (1500–1750)			
Wolfgang Capito	1478–1541	Nonclerical	Mostly a professor and cathedral preacher
Andreas R. B. von Karlstadt	1486–1541	Nonclerical	Held teaching positions at Wittenberg and Basel
Johann Oecolampadius	1482–1531	Nonclerical	Studied law and theology, held various teaching positions
Martin Luther	1483–1546	Nonclerical	Monk, professor of theology at Wittenberg
Ulrich Zwingli	1484–1531	Clerical	Minister in Zurich
Joachim Vadianus	1484–1551	Nonclerical	Humanist, physician, held teaching position
Johannes Bugenhagen	1485–1558	Clerical	Rector at Wittenberg, Luther's pastor

Reformation to Enlightenment (1500 – 1750) continued			
Philipp Melanchthon	1497 – 1560	Nonclerical	Professor of Greek at Wittenberg
Thomas Cranmer	1489 – 1556	Clerical	English cleric, founding father of English Protestant church
Guillaume Farel	1489 – 1565	Clerical	French Reformer, pastor of Neuchatel
Martin Bucer	1491 – 1551	Nonclerical	Ecclesiastical adviser, professor at Cambridge
Justus Jonas	1493 – 1555	Nonclerical	Taught law and theology, involved in church reform
William Tyndale	1494 – 1536	Nonclerical	Bible translator
John Hooper	d. 1555	Clerical	Bishop of Gloucester and Worchester
John Bale	1495 – 1563	Clerical	Bishop of Ossory
Wolfgang Musculus	1497 – 1563	Clerical	Monk, then pastor at Church of the Holy Cross
Jan Laski	1499 – 1560	Clerical	Polish Calvinist Reformer, held various church positions
Pietro Martire Vermigli	1499 – 1562	Nonclerical	Florentine humanist, then professor at Oxford
Johannes Brenz	1499 – 1570	Clerical	Leading clergyman of the Lutheran church in Württemberg
Nicholas Ridley	1500 – 1555	Clerical	Bishop of London and Protestant martyr
Erasmus Sarcerius	1501 – 1559	Clerical	Lutheran educator, pastor in Leipzig
Georg Major	1502 – 1574	Nonclerical	Professor at the University of Wittenberg
John Frith	1503 – 1533	Nonclerical	English Reformer, associate of Tyndale, martyr

Reformation to Enlightenment (1500 – 1750) continued			
Heinrich Bullinger	1504 – 1575	Clerical	Succeeded Zwingli as the chief pastor at Zurich
Augustin Marlorat	1506 – 1562	Clerical	Monk until 1535, then became Protestant pastor near Lausanne
John Calvin	1509 – 1564	Clerical	Pastor at Geneva and church reformer
John Bradford	1510 – 1555	Nonclerical	Worked job in English army, became a professor
Immanuel Tremellius	1510 – 1580	Nonclerical	Biblical scholar and teacher
Michael Servetus	1511 – 1553	Nonclerical	Physician and Unitarian theologian
Andreas Hyperius	1511 – 1564	Nonclerical	Professor who lectured on theology
Pierre Viret	1511 – 1571	Clerical	Swiss Protestant minister, popular preacher
Thomas Becon	1512 – 1567	Clerical	English Protestant propagandist and popular preacher
S. Castellion	1515 – 1563	Nonclerical	Professor of Greek at Basel, spent most of his life as teacher
Petrus Ramus	1515 – 1572	Nonclerical	French humanist, professor before and after conversion
John Philpot	1516 – 1555	Nonclerical	French humanist, teacher at different universities
Edwin Sandys	1516 – 1588	Clerical	Anglican Bishop of Worchester
Girolamo Zanchi	1516 – 1590	Nonclerical	Professor at Strasbourg and Heidelberg

Reformation to Enlightenment (1500 – 1750) continued			
Edmund Grindal	1519 – 1583	Clerical	Successively Bishop of London, Archbishop of York, then Canterbury
Rudolph Gwalther	1519 – 1586	Clerical	Third Antistes (or Bishop) of the Reformed Church of Zurich
James Pilkington	1520 – 1576	Clerical	Bishop of Durham
Johann Wolf	1521 – 1571	Nonclerical	German Christian Hebraist, later became professor at Hamburg
John Jewel	1522 – 1571	Clerical	Bishop of Salisbury
Martin Chemnitz	1522 – 1586	Clerical	Professor, then superintendent of Braunschweig churches
Johann Wigand	1523 – 1587	Clerical	Various pastoral jobs
Ludwig Lavater	1527 – 1586	Clerical	Archdeacon at Zurich
Tilemann Heshusius	1527 – 1588	Nonclerical	Lutheran lecturer on rhetoric and theology at Heidelberg
Jakob Andreae	1528 – 1590	Nonclerical	Lutheran Reformer, ecclesiastical diplomat, various occupations
James Calfhill	1530 – 1570	Clerical	Various, then Archdeacon of Colchester in 1565
Josias Simmler	1530 – 1576	Nonclerical	Pastored in Zurich, then professor at Zurich Academy
Lambert Daneau	1530 – 1595	Clerical	French Calvinist pastor
John Whitgift	1532 – 1604	Clerical	English prelate, Archbishop of Canterbury for twenty years
David Chytraeus	1531 – 1600	Nonclerical	German Lutheran theologian, professor at University of Rostock

Reformation to Enlightenment (1500 – 1750) continued			
Zacharias Ursinus	1534 – 1583	Clerical	Taught Latin in Breslau, professor and rector of a seminary
Antoine de Chandieu	1534 – 1591	Clerical	Pastor in Geneva while teaching Hebrew in the Geneva academy
John Woolton	1535 – 1594	Clerical	Bishop of Exeter
Thomas Cartwright	1535 – 1603	Clerical	Professor at Trinity College, then Presbyterian minister
Caspar Olevian	1536 – 1587	Nonclerical	Taught at University of Heidelberg
William Fulke	1538 – 1589	Nonclerical	Puritan, lecturer, and preacher, then chaplain to Earl of Leicester
Faustus Socinus	1539 – 1604	Nonclerical	Supported by a wealthy patron, wrote theological works
Christoph Pezel	1539 – 1604	Nonclerical	Professor of philosophy, then ordained preacher at Wittenberg
Gellius Snecanus	1540 – 1596	Clerical	Catholic priest, then minister in Reformed church
Franciscus Junius	1545 – 1602	Nonclerical	Pastor and army chaplain, then professor of theology at Neustadt
Johannes Piscator	1546 – 1625	Nonclerical	Professor of theology at Strasbourg, Neustadt, and Herborn
William Whitaker	1548 – 1595	Nonclerical	Professor at Cambridge
David Pareus	1548 – 1622	Clerical	Pastor at Niedersclettenbach, then teacher at Heidelberg, then pastor
John Rainolds	1549 – 1607	Nonclerical	Professor at Oxford

Reformation to Enlightenment (1500 – 1750) continued			
Aegidius Hunnius	1550 – 1603	Nonclerical	Taught at Marburg
Jeremias Bastingius	1551 – 1595	Clerical	Pastor in Antwerp and Dordrecht, briefly professor at Leiden
Robert Rollock	1555 – 1599	Clerical	Professor of theology, minister in the Edinburgh
William Temple	1555 – 1627	Nonclerical	Professor throughout lifetime
Sibrand Lubbert	1556 – 1625	Nonclerical	Professor of theology at Franeker
Dudley Fenner	1558 – 1587	Clerical	Preacher in Antwerp, then rest of life as chaplain in Reformed church
William Perkins	1558 – 1602	Nonclerical	Fellow at Christ's College, Cambridge
Jacobus Arminius	1560 – 1609	Clerical	Reformed pastor in Amsterdam, theologian at Leiden
Amandus P. von Polansdorf	1561 – 1610	Nonclerical	Professor of Old Testament in Basel
Hans Poulsen Resen	1561 – 1638	Clerical	Professor of theology at Copenhagen, then Bishop of Zealand
Andrew Willet	1562 – 1621	Clerical	Spent most of his life as minister
Leonard Hutter	1563 – 1616	Nonclerical	Professor of theology at Wittenberg
F. Gomarus	1563 – 1641	Nonclerical	Professor at Leiden, then Groningen
Wolfgang Franz	1564 – 1628	Nonclerical	Professor at Wittenberg
Daniel Chamier	1565 – 1621	Clerical	Pastor and professor at Montauban

Reformation to Enlightenment (1500 – 1750) continued			
Pierre DeMoulin	1568 – 1658	Nonclerical	Huguenot minister, prebendary at Canterbury Cathedral, then professor
Conradus Vorstius	1569 – 1622	Nonclerical	Professor at Steinfurt, replaced J. Arminius in his position later
Lucas Trelcatius	1570 – 1607	Nonclerical	Professor at Leiden with J. Arminius, then died of plague
Bartholomaus Keckermann	1571 – 1608	Nonclerical	Taught Hebrew at Heidelberg, then returned to Danzig to teach
William Bradshaw	1571 – 1618	Nonclerical	English Puritan and separatist, fellow of Sidney Sussex College
Henry Ainsworth	1571 – 1622	Clerical	English nonconformist clergyman and scholar
Valentin Smalcius	1572 – 1622	Nonclerical	Taught at various Polish schools
Matthias Martini	1572 – 1630	Nonclerical	Court preacher at Dillenburg, then professor at Herborn
John Davenant	1572 – 1641	Clerical	President of Queens College Cambridge, Bishop of Salisbury
Andre Rivet	1572 – 1651	Clerical	Pastor, then professor at Leiden
Antonius Walaeus	1573 – 1639	Clerical	Pastor at Dutch Reformed Church, then taught at Middelburg
Thomas Gataker	1574 – 1654	Clerical	Preacher to the Society of Lincoln's Inn
Joseph Hall	1574 – 1656	Clerical	Bishop of Norwich
William Ames	1576 – 1633	Nonclerical	English Calvinist, professor at Franeker

Reformation to Enlightenment (1500 – 1750) continued			
Festus Hommius	1576 – 1642	Clerical	Dutch Calvinist minister at Reformed Church at Leiden
Jean Diodati	1576 – 1642	Nonclerical	Professor of theology
Richard Sibbes	1577 – 1635	Nonclerical	Professor at Cambridge
Gerardus Joannes Vossius	1577 – 1649	Nonclerical	Professor of rhetoric, history, and politics
William Twisse	1578 – 1646	Clerical	Prolocutor of the Westminster Assembly, clergyman and theologian
John Prideaux	1578 – 1650	Clerical	English academic, Bishop of Worcester, helped in church reform
William Gouge	1578 – 1653	Clerical	Preacher at St. Ann Blackfriars for 45 years
John Weemes	1579 – 1636	Clerical	Church of England minister, biblical exegete
Thomas Jackson	1579 – 1640	Nonclerical	President of college at Oxford
George Walker	1581 – 1651	Clerical	English clergyman, Westminster Assembly of Divines
John Downame	? – 1652	Clerical	Ordained minister, various church positions
James Ussher	1581 – 1656	Clerical	Church of Ireland Archbishop and scholar
Johann Gerhard	1582 – 1637	Nonclerical	Taught theology at Jena
Simon Episcopius	1583 – 1643	Nonclerical	Professor of theology at Leiden
Hugo Grotius	1583 – 1645	Nonclerical	Dutch jurist and Christian humanist
Edward Herbert	1583 – 1648	Nonclerical	Philosopher and poet

Reformation to Enlightenment (1500 – 1750) continued			
Jacobus Trigland	1583 – 1654	Clerical	Dutch Reformed minister, then theology professor at Leiden
David Dickson	1583 – 1663	Clerical	Professor, then minister
Nicolaus Hunnius	1585 – 1643	Nonclerical	Lutheran theologian and professor
Jesper Rasumussen Brochmand	1585 – 1652	Clerical	Professor and Bishop of Zealand
Louis Cappel	1585 – 1658	Nonclerical	Professor at Oxford
Matthew Wren	1585 – 1667	Clerical	Various, then Bishop of Hereford, Norwich, and Ely
Johannes Wolleb	1586 – 1629	Clerical	Minister at Basel Cathedral
Thomas Hooker	1586 – 1647	Clerical	Pastor in England, then took congregation to America
Georg Calixt	1586 – 1656	Nonclerical	Professor of theology at Helmstedt
Miles Coverdale	1488 – 1568	Clerical	Bishop and Bible translator
Johann Heinrich Alsted	1588 – 1638	Nonclerical	Professor of theology and philosophy
Jan Makowski	1588 – 1644	Nonclerical	Professor at Franeker for many years
Johann Crell	1590 – 1633	Nonclerical	Worked at Racovian Academy, a socian theologian
Franco Burgersdijck	1590 – 1635	Nonclerical	Professor at Leiden
Richard Holdsworth	1590 – 1649	Nonclerical	Held many posts in university settings
Johannes Cloppenburg	1592 – 1652	Nonclerical	Professor at various universities

Reformation to Enlightenment (1500 – 1750) continued			
Robert Baron	1593 – 1639	Nonclerical	Professor of divinity
Salomon Glass	1593 – 1656	Clerical	Professor, then superintendent in Sondershausen
Abraham Heidanus	1597 – 1678	Clerical	Dutch Calvinist minister involved in church reform, then professor
Jeremiah Burroughs	1599 – 1646	Clerical	Puritan preacher and English Congregationalist
Johann Buxtorf	1599 – 1664	Nonclerical	University professor
Anthony Tuckney	1599 – 1670	Nonclerical	Chairman of Westminster Assembly, professor of divinity
Samuel Maresius	1599 – 1673	Clerical	Priest, university professor, then pastor
Friedrich Spanheim	1600 – 1649	Nonclerical	University professor
Brian Walton	1600 – 1661	Clerical	Rector in London and Essex, Bishop of Chester
Samuel Rutherford	1600 – 1661	Clerical	Professor, then pastor
Thomas Goodwin	1600 – 1680	Clerical	Various duties, pastor
John Arrowsmith	1602 – 1659	Nonclerical	English theologian and university professor
Herbert Croft	1603 – 1691	Clerical	Bishop of Hereford
Edward Pococke	1604 – 1691	Nonclerical	Ordained priest, university chair, historian
Francis Cheynell	1608 – 1665	Clerical	Chaplain, vicar, rector
Francis Roberts	1609 – 1675	Clerical	Parish minister, librarian
Daniel Zwicker	1612 – 1678	Nonclerical	Medical doctor, writer
Abraham Calov	1612 – 1686	Nonclerical	University professor

Reformation to Enlightenment (1500–1750) continued			
George Ashwell	1612–1695	Clerical	Rector, chaplain
George Gillespie	1613–1648	Clerical	Minister in Fife, member of Glasgow Assembly
William Jenkyn	1613–1685	Clerical	Presbyterian minister
John Pearson	1613–1689	Nonclerical	Chaplain, then preacher, later professor at Cambridge
Henry More	1614–1687	Nonclerical	Fellow at Christ's College, prebend in Gloucester Cathedral
John Biddle	1615–1662	Nonclerical	Headmaster of Crypt Grammar School, biblical scholar
Richard Baxter	1615–1691	Clerical	Reformed Pastor
John Owen	1616–1683	Clerical	Renowned preacher and pastor, later vice chancellor at Oxford
Johannes Hoornbeeck	1617–1666	Nonclerical	Theology professor
Patrick Gillespie	1617–1675	Clerical	Scottish minister, then principal at University of Glasgow
Johann Andreas Quenstedt	1617–1688	Nonclerical	Professor at Wittenberg
Ralph Cudworth	1617–1688	Nonclerical	Professor at Emmanuel college, later Christ's College
Seth Ward	1617–1689	Clerical	Bishop of Exeter, Salisbury
Sebastian Schmid	1617–1696	Nonclerical	Professor of theology
Isaac Vossius	1618–1689	Nonclerical	Manuscript scholar
Thomas Manton	1620–1677	Clerical	Puritan preacher/ minister

Reformation to Enlightenment (1500 – 1750) continued			
Samuel Annesley	1620 – 1696	Clerical	Puritan pastor
Thomas Long	1621 – 1707	Clerical	Prebend of Exeter
Fran Turrettini	1623 – 1687	Clerical	French pastor
Matthew Poole	1624 – 1679	Nonclerical	Theologian, lived off patrimony
George Fox	1624 – 1691	Nonclerical	Lay-preacher, Quaker leader
Arthur Bury	1624 – 1713	Nonclerical	Rector at Exeter in Oxford
Christoph Wittich	1625 – 1687	Nonclerical	Philosophy, math, and Hebrew professor
William Bates	1625 – 1699	Clerical	Presbyterian minister
Gilbert Clerke	1626 – 1697	Nonclerical	Private scholar and mathematician
Stephen Charnock	1628 – 1680	Clerical	Primarily worked as a preacher and chaplain in Dublin
Johannes Braun	1628 – 1708	Nonclerical	Theology professor
John Howe	1630 – 1705	Clerical	Rector, chaplain, various positions
Lancelot Addison	1632 – 1703	Clerical	Royal chaplain, rector, dean of Lichfield
Edward Burrough	1634 – 1662	Nonclerical	Quaker leader and preacher
Edmund Elys	1634 – 1707	Clerical	Rector, sympathies with the Quakers
Robert South	1634 – 1716	Nonclerical	Professor and preacher, but primarily in university contexts
Edward Stillingfleet	1635 – 1699	Clerical	Preacher and vicar of St. Andrew, later Bishop of Worcester

Reformation to Enlightenment (1500 – 1750) continued			
Leonard van Rijssen	1636 – ?	Clerical	Occupied various pastorates
Herman Witsius	1636 – 1708	Clerical	Various pastoral positions, appointed professor of divinity in 1675
George Whitehead	1636 – 1723	Nonclerical	Traveling lay preacher, writer, lobbyist
William Cave	1637 – 1713	Nonclerical	Chaplain, spent most of his life in private reflection and study
John Edwards	1637 – 1716	Nonclerical	Professor, moderator, college fellow
August Pfeiffer	1640 – 1698	Clerical	Occupied various pastorates as well as academic positions
William Sherlock	1641 – 1707	Clerical	Rector at St. George's Cathedral and dean at St. Paul's in London
Pierre Allix	1641 – 1717	Clerical	Pastor at various posts in France, and later in London
Melchior Leydekker	1642 – 1721	Nonclerical	Began career as a pastor, then held university posts for rest of his life
Gilbert Burnet	1643 – 1715	Clerical	Bishop of Salisbury, renowned preacher and linguist
Christoph Sand	1644 – 1680	Nonclerical	Editor, writer, publisher in Amsterdam
William Basset	1644 – 1695	Clerical	Rector in London
Stephen Lobb	1647 – 1699	Clerical	English nonconformist minister, later court minister
Thomas Watson	1620 – 1686	Clerical	Pastor and preacher

Reformation to Enlightenment (1500 – 1750) continued			
Robert Barclay	1648 – 1690	Nonclerical	Quaker politician and scholar
Stephen Nye	1648 – 1719	Clerical	Rector in Hertfordshire
Samuel Bold	1649 – 1737	Clerical	Rector, preacher, controversialist
H. C. DeLuzancy	? – 1713	Clerical	Deacon of the church of England, also professor at Christ Church
Charles Leslie	1650 – 1722	Nonclerical	Justice of the Peace, lay writer
Benedict Pictet	1655 – 1724	Clerical	Both pastor and theology professor
Johannes Marck	1656 – 1731	Nonclerical	Professor at various universities
William Nicholls	1664 – 1712	Clerical	Rector, author of the Book of Common Prayer
		C-102, NC-98	

The Digital Library of the Catholic Reformation

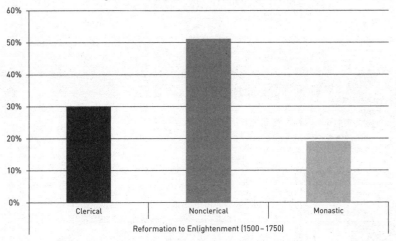

Ratio of Clerical, Nonclerical, and Monastic Theologians in
The Digital Library of the Catholic Reformation

Classification of Authors in
The Digital Library of The Catholic Reformation

Reformation to Enlightenment (1500–1750) continued			
Desiderius Erasmus	1466–1536	Nonclerical	Priest, professor, writer
Jacques Lefevre d'Etaples	?–1536	Nonclerical	Scholar, secretary
Josse Clichtove	?–1543	Nonclerical	Librarian, teacher, secretary
Friedrich Nausea	?–1552	Clerical	Bishop
Roger Edgeworth	?–1560	Clerical	Preacher, priest, professor
Thomas Dorman	?–1577	Nonclerical	Professor
Jean Benedicti	?–1611	Monastic	Monastic
John Gother	?–1704	Clerical	Priest, preacher, chaplain

Reformation to Enlightenment (1500–1750) continued			
Johann Geiler von Kaysersberg	1445–1510	Clerical	Priest, preacher
Girolamo Savonarola	1452–1498	Monastic	Friar, priest, preacher
Johann Reuchlin	1455–1522	Nonclerical	professor, scholar
Sebastian Brant	1458–1521	Nonclerical	Professor
Richard Bristow	1458–1521	Nonclerical	Author, scholar
Jacobus van Hoogstraten	1460–1527	Nonclerical	Monastic, scholar
Johannes Trithemius	1462–1516	Monastic	Abbot, scholar
Kaspar Schatzgeyer	1464–1527	Monastic	Franciscan
Bartholomaeus Arnoldi	1465–1532	Nonclerical	Professor
John Colet	1467–1519	Nonclerical	Scholar, professor, preacher
Tommaso de Vio Cajetan	1469–1534	Clerical	Cardinal
John Fisher	1469–1535	Clerical	Cardinal, bishop
Lorenzo Campeggio	1474–1539	Clerical	Cardinal
Thomas Murner	1475–1537	Nonclerical	Professor, writer, poet
Johann Dietenberger	c. 1475–1537	Nonclerical	Professor
Jacopo Sadoleto	1477–1547	Clerical	Cardinal, bishop
Hieronymus Emser	1478–1527	Nonclerical	Professor
Thomas More	1478–1535	Nonclerical	Statesman

Reformation to Enlightenment (1500 – 1750) continued			
Johannes Cochlaeus	1479 – 1552	Clerical	Writer, secular priest
Leandro Alberti	1479 – 1552	Nonclerical	Professor, historian
Carolus Bovillus	1479 – 1567	Nonclerical	Writer, mathematician
Arnaldus Albertinus	1480 – 1544	Clerical	Inquisitor, Bishop of Patti
Tommaso Campeggi	1483 – 1564	Clerical	Bishop
Johann Eck	1486 – 1543	Nonclerical	Writer
Johannes Justus Lansperger	1489 – 1539	Nonclerical	Monastic
Albertus Pighius	c. 1490 – 1542	Nonclerical	Scholar, statesman
Ignatius of Loyola	1491 – 1556	Monastic	Founder of the Society of Jesus (Jesuits)
Juan Luis Vives	1492 – 1540	Nonclerical	Professor, scholar
Domingo de Soto	1494 – 1560	Nonclerical	Dominican university professor
Johannes Mensing	1495 – 1541	Clerical	Monastic provincial, then Bishop of Halberstadt
Giovanni Matteo Giberti	1495 – 1543	Clerical	Bishop
Bartolomeo Camerario	1497 – 1564	Nonclerical	Professor
Gaspar de Loarte	1498 – 1578	Monastic	Jesuit, spiritual writer
Gentian Hervet	1499 – 1584	Clerical	Professor, secretary, priest
John of Avila	1499? – 1569	Clerical	Priest, preacher
Luis de Carvajal	1500 – 1552	Nonclerical	Franciscan professor at Paris
Reginald Pole	1500 – 1558	Clerical	Archbishop

Reformation to Enlightenment (1500 – 1750) continued			
Edmund Bonner	1500 – 1569	Clerical	Bishop
Lodovico Beccadelli	1502 – 1572	Clerical	Bishop
Johann Faber	1504 – 1558	Clerical	Bishop
Stanislaw Hozjusz	1504 – 1579	Clerical	Bishop
Luis de Granada	1504 – 1588	Monastic	Dominican scholar and Friar
Francis Xavier	1506 – 1552	Monastic	Jesuit missionary
Michael Helding	1506 – 1561	Clerical	Bishop
Louis de Blois	1506 – 1566	Monastic	Benedictine abbot in Hainaut
Giovanni Gerolamo Albani	1509 – 1591	Nonclerical	Professor, scholar
Melchor Cano	1509? – 1560	Nonclerical	Scholastic (bishop later in life)
Claude d' Espence	1511 – 1571	Nonclerical	Rector at University of Paris
George Cassander	1513 – 1566	Nonclerical	Professor
Michael Bajus	1513 – 1589	Nonclerical	Professor, chancellor
Simon Vigor	1515 – 1575	Clerical	Bishop
Teresa of Avila	1515 – 1582	Monastic	Nun, mystic
Thomas Harding	1516 – 1572	Clerical	Priest, chaplain, prebendary of Winchester
Nicholas Harpsfield	1519 – 1575	Clerical	Archdeacon of Canterbury
Laurence Vaux	1519 – 1585	Monastic	Sub-prior of St. Martin's
Petrus Canisius	1521 – 1597	Monastic	Jesuit teacher

Reformation to Enlightenment (1500–1750) continued			
Laurentius Surius	1522–1578	Monastic	Monastic, Carthusian Monastery in Cologne
Pedro de Ribadeneyra	1526–1611	Monastic	Jesuit teacher and missionary
Domingo Banez	1528–1604	Nonclerical	Professor-teacher
Onofrio Panvinio	1529–1568	Nonclerical	Librarian
Nicholas Sander	1530–1581	Clerical	Priest
Emond Auger	1530–1591	Nonclerical	Royal confessor
Lorenzo Scupoli	1530–1610	Monastic	Theatines
Agostino Valiero	1531–1606	Clerical	Bishop, cardinal
John Rastell	1532–1577	Monastic	Jesuit teacher
William Allen	1532–1594	Clerical	Librarian, cardinal
Franciscus Coster	1532–1619	Monastic	Jesuit provincial
Johannes Molanus	1533–1585	Nonclerical	Professor, headmaster
John Martiall	1534–1597	Nonclerical	Professor
Antonio Possevino	1534–1611	Nonclerical	Secretary, scholar
Thomas Stapleton	1535–1598	Nonclerical	Professor, college founder
Juan de Mariana	1535–1624	Clerical	Priest, historian
Cesare Baronio	1538–1607	Clerical	Cardinal, historian
Adam Blackwood	1539–1613	Nonclerical	Rector at University of Paris, lawyer
Edmund Campion	1540–1581	Monastic	English Jesuit missionary
Alfonso Chacon	1530–1599	Nonclerical	Dominican scholar in Rome

Reformation to Enlightenment (1500 – 1750) continued			
Giovanni Botero	1540 – 1617	Nonclerical	Secretary, diplomat, priest
Gregory Martin	1542 – 1582	Nonclerical	Translator
John of the Cross	1542 – 1591	Monastic	Mystic, Carmelite friar
Luca Pinellli	1542 – 1607	Nonclerical	Professor, teacher
Robert F. R. Bellarmino	1542 – 1621	Clerical	Cardinal
Claudio Acquaviva	1543 – 1615	Monastic	General of the Jesuits
John Gibbons	1544 – 1589	Nonclerical	Confessor, professor
William Rainolds	1544 – 1594	Nonclerical	Professor, chaplain
Angelo Rocca	1545 – 1620	Nonclerical	Librarian, sacristan
Robert Parsons	1546 – 1610	Monastic	English Jesuit missionary
Francisco Suarez	1548 – 1617	Nonclerical	Priest, professor, theology chair
Nicholas Fitzherbert	1550 – 1612	Nonclerical	Secretary, scholar
Richard Verstegan	1550 – 1640	Nonclerical	Confessor, author
Thomas Alfield	1552 – 1585	Clerical	Priest, Catholic martyr in England
Leonardus Lessius	1554 – 1623	Nonclerical	Professor
Henry Garnet	1555 – 1606	Nonclerical	Professor, secretary, priest
William Watson	1559 – 1603	Clerical	Priest and political conspirator
Robert Southwell	1561 – 1595	Monastic	English Jesuit missionary
Thomas Wright	1561 – 1623	Nonclerical	Writer
Jakob Gretser	1562 – 1625	Nonclerical	Professor, writer

Reformation to Enlightenment (1500 – 1750) continued			
Martinus Becanus	1563 – 1624	Nonclerical	Professor, writer, priest, confessor
Pierre Coton	1564 – 1626	Monastic	French Jesuit priest, confessor
Federico Borremeo	1564 – 1631	Clerical	Cardinal, archbishop
Francis de Sales	1567 – 1622	Clerical	Bishop
Cornelius Cornelii Lapide	1567 – 1637	Nonclerical	Professor
Richard Smith	1568 – 1655	Clerical	Bishop
Etienne Binet	1569 – 1639	Nonclerical	Writer
Anthony Champney	1569 – 1643	Nonclerical	College president, Fellow of the Sorbonne
Adam Contzen	1571 – 1635	Nonclerical	Professor, chancellor
Pierre de Berulle	1575 – 1629	Clerical	Statesman, priest, cardinal
Antonio Bosio	1575 – 1629	Nonclerical	Scholar, historian, archeologist
Jean Duvergier de Hauranne	1581 – 1643	Monastic	Abbot, scholar
John Barclay	1582 – 1621	Nonclerical	Writer, poet
Nicolas Caussin	1583 – 1651	Nonclerical	Confessor, philosopher
Denis Petau	1583 – 1652	Nonclerical	Professor
Francois Garasse	1584 – 1631	Nonclerical	Professor
Jean-Pierre Camus	1584 – 1652	Clerical	Preacher, bishop
Cornelius Jansenius	1585 – 1638	Clerical	Bishop
Armand Jean du Plessis Richelieu	1585 – 1642	Clerical	Bishop, cardinal

Reformation to Enlightenment (1500–1750) continued			
Antonino Diana	1585–1663	Nonclerical	Examiner, confessor
Libert Froidmont	1587–1653	Nonclerical	Professor
Valeriano Magni	1587–1661	Monastic	Missionary
Luke Wadding	1588–1657	Nonclerical	Founder of Franciscan colleges
Jean Morin	1591–1659	Nonclerical	Priest, writer
Francisco de Macedo	1596–1681	Nonclerical	Professor, secretary
Kenelm Digby	1603–1665	Nonclerical	Statesman, diplomat
Louis Abelly	1604–1691	Clerical	Priest, bishop
Jean-Jacques Olier	1608–1657	Clerical	Parish priest, founder of seminary
Antoine Arnauld	1612–1694	Nonclerical	Professor
Blaise Pascal	1623–1662	Nonclerical	Professor, scholar, philosopher
Pierre Nicole	1625–1695	Nonclerical	Teacher, writer, publisher
Jacques Benigne Bossuet	1627–1704	Clerical	Preacher, bishop
Louis Bourdaloue	1632–1704	Monastic	French Jesuit priest
Jean Mabillon	1632–1707	Nonclerical	Benedictine scholar and professor
Richard Simon	1638–1712	Nonclerical	Preacher, professor, priest
Jean Marie Bouvier	1648–1717	Monastic	Nun, mystic
		C-42, NC-71, M-27	

Index

Also by Gerald Hiestand and Todd Wilson

Gerald Hiestand

Sex, Dating and Relationships: A Fresh Approach

Todd Wilson

Real Christian: Bearing the Marks of Authentic Faith

Galatians: Gospel-Rooted Living

Pastors in the Classics: Timeless Lessons on Life and Ministry
from World Literature *(with Leland Ryken and Philip Ryken)*